COLD-BLOODED KILLINGS

KILLINGS

Hits, assassinations and near misses that shook the world

Charlotte Greig

Capella

Pictures reproduced with the permission of the following picture agencies:

Corbis: 7, 9, 10, 12, 13, 14, 15, 18, 21, 24, 27, 28, 30, 33, 35, 36, 39, 40, 45, 47, 49, 50, 54, 61, 62, 65, 67, 68, 70, 72, 75, 77, 79, 81, 82, 84, 91, 92, 94, 98, 101, 102, 104, 108, 111, 112, 115, 119, 120, 123, 124, 127, 130, 133, 136, 138, 143, 148, 149, 150, 153, 154, 156, 159, 160, 162, 164, 166, 170, 172, 181, 185, 188, 190, 194, 198, 204, 207

Lebrecht: 23, 86, 200, 201

Rex: 17, 42, 46, 58, 93, 106, 116, 118, 128, 134, 140, 147, 173, 176, 178, 182

This edition published in 2006 by Arcturus Publishing Limited
26/27 Bickels Yard, 151–153 Bermondsey Street,
London SE1 3HA

ISBN-13: 978-1-84193-405-1
ISBN-10: 1-84193-405-4

This edition printed in 2006
Copyright © 2006 Arcturus Publishing Limited

British Library Cataloguing-in-Publication Data: a catalogue record for this
book is available from the British Library

Printed in China

CONTENTS

INTRODUCTION

Throughout history, assassinations of famous figures, whether major political leaders, powerful business people, or celebrities from the world of entertainment, have shocked onlookers, the media and the general public. These sudden, brutal killings have the dual purpose of murdering a well-known figure, thus putting an end to his or her influence, and also drawing attention to a political, religious, or social issue that may have been ignored or overlooked up to that point. Yet, as it transpires, a large number of assassinations are committed by people whose political affiliations are questionable; and in some cases, assassins have no political affiliations whatsoever.

What characterizes almost all of them, however, is an element of fanaticism. Many assassins are young men, often aged between eighteen and twenty-two, whose sense of mortality and caution is lacking; others are mentally unstable, often with a history of anti-social behaviour and consequent social exclusion; and yet others show signs of serious mental illness, to the point where their grasp of reality is so tenuous that they suffer from delusions, and they become extremely dangerous, violent individuals. Interestingly, there are very few instances where assassinations take place as a result of rational, pre-meditated plans on the part of political opponents. In most cases, even where the target is an oppressive ruler, assassinations appear to be committed in a random way, by people with disordered, impressionable minds, rather than being the outcome of carefully planned actions by ruthless, intelligent people determined to rid themselves of a political opponent.

Over the centuries, assassination has been used as a political weapon by pressure groups, often with far-reaching consequences that affect millions of people around the world. But there have also been many assassinations by lone individuals who are mentally unbalanced in some way. These have also, in many cases, had a profound effect on our lives, and cause us to reflect on the sanity of our modern-day society, in which security has become such a major issue.

The great assassinations

In this book, we look at the political assassinations that have shaped our history: for example, the assassination of Archduke Ferdinand on 28 June 1914, which heralded the outbreak of the First World War; the assassination of President John F. Kennedy on 22 November 1963, a date still etched in many people's minds as they remember what they were doing when they first heard the news; and the assassination of Martin Luther King on 4 April 1968, whose murder had wide-ranging consequences for the progress of civil rights and race relations in the US and around the world. The assassination of other important world leaders, both contemporary and historical, is included too, from Julius Caesar to Mahatma Gandhi, from Patrice Lumumba to Yitzhak Rabin.

We also include the assassinations of maverick figures who achieved fame – or notoriety – in their times: those such as Rasputin, the drunken womanizer who became a friend to the Russian royal family, and who was believed to have magical powers; or Jean-Paul Marat, the bloodthirsty French revolutionary who made lists of those he wanted sent to the guillotine while he was in his bath, and who was brutally stabbed to death by a young radical, Charlotte Corday. In more recent times, there was flamboyant gay Dutch politician Pim Fortuyn, who was shot to death in a car park by a lone gunman. Then there are the chilling assassinations such as that of the ousted Bolshevik leader Leon Trotsky, who met his death with an ice pick embedded in his head; or Georgi Markov, the Bulgarian émigré who was stabbed with a poisoned umbrella while walking on Waterloo Bridge, and who died in agony several days later.

Celebrity hits…and misses

In addition to these killings, we also deal with the assassinations of famous figures from the world of music, film and fashion, such as John Lennon and Gianni Versace. Often, the motives for these murders remain shadowy: they may be to do with the disturbed psychology of the assassin, who at once hero-worships and hates his idol; or there may be a web of circumstances underlying the murder that still, to this day, has not been fully investigated. Whatever the case, it seems that murders of celebrity

The 'mad monk' of Romanov Russia, Rasputin was not easily assassinated. He was poisoned, shot and eventually drowned

figures are usually committed by people with extremely unbalanced minds, whose own frustrations and anxieties have reached a pitch where they are no longer in control of their actions – with devastating consequences for their innocent victims. Certainly, it seems true to say that in our modern-day culture, the mere fact of being a celebrity makes one vulnerable to abuse from all kinds of mentally disturbed individuals, whether this abuse is harassment, stalking or – in the worst case – murder.

Of course, the history of assassinations is not just one of 'hits'. In this book, we also take a look at the assassinations that failed: the 'near misses', which are almost more fascinating than the hits. These are the attempted assassinations of political leaders like Adolf Hitler, Ronald Reagan, Charles de Gaulle and Margaret Thatcher, as well as cultural icons like Andy Warhol. What led to these crazed attempts? What stopped them? What would have happened if they'd pulled them off? And, most intriguingly, how did figures such as Reagan, de Gaulle, and Thatcher manage to remain so remarkably calm in the face of these attacks?

High drama

As well as discussing the implications of assassinations, we also go into detail as to the events themselves. Assassinations are, of course, usually highly dramatic events. Take the assassination of Julius Caesar, for instance, the Roman emperor who, at the height of his power, was stabbed to death in the Senate by a group of conspirators he thought were his friends and followers. Or that of Thomas Becket, the twelfth century archbishop and head of the British church who was stabbed to death by four heavily armed knights at Canterbury Cathedral as he stood on the steps of the altar, in full view of the congregation during a church service. Both these stories inspired many poets, writers and dramatists. In Shakespeare's play, *Julius Caesar*, the emperor speaks the immortal lines, 'Et tu, Brute', on seeing the young man he believed to be his friend (or, as some believe, his son) coming forward to strike him. Today, Shakespeare's saying is

used to describe anger and dismay at the treachery of a friend. In the same way, the brutal slaying of Thomas Becket was dramatized by T.S. Eliot in *Murder in the Cathedral*, one of literature's most celebrated works.

There are many other instances of dramatic assassinations, such as that of Patrice Lumumba, the deposed prime minister of the Congo, ambushed as he tried to escape from his captors, and shot by a firing squad on the side of a road; or that of Park Chung Hee, gunned down while he was attending a secret meeting with his aides, in a bloody shoot-out worthy of a cop movie script. In all of them, there is a sense of unreality, when, suddenly, everyday life turns into a nightmare. For example, the assassination of Alexander II of Russia, when the cheering crowd is silenced as an explosion rips apart the Czar's carriage, leaving blood, flesh and debris hanging from the trees; or the assassination of Louis Mountbatten, when a family outing in a boat, sailing out into the calm blue seas of an Irish bay on a beautiful summer's day, turns to tragedy as a bomb detonates, and the boat splinters apart, like matchsticks thrown into the air. Or that of Olof Palme, walking quietly with his wife through the streets of Stockholm after a trip to the cinema, only to be confronted by a gunman and shot in cold blood at point blank range.

The targets

As well as describing and analyzing the assassination events themselves, we also profile the figures who have met their deaths in this way, providing insights into

Gandhi's assassination sent shock waves around the world – an appalling ending for such a peace-loving man

background and career. All these are famous people who have made their name as leaders in the world of politics, religion, entertainment or art. In every case, their lives are exciting, and provide a fascinating testament to the places and times they lived in: whether popular spiritual leaders like the Indian premier Mahatma Gandhi; swashbuckling men of action like the Mexican revolutionary Pancho Villa; feared and hated oppressors like the eighteenth-century Jacobin Jean-Paul Marat, known as 'the butcher'; or admired celebrities from the glittering world of fashion and entertainment, like Gianni Versace. In addition, we look at the lives of those who were constantly under threat

from would-be assassins, but somehow – through courage, intelligence, and sheer good luck – managed to escape with their lives: the impetuous Elizabeth I, Queen of England; the urbane King Hussein of Jordan; and the iconic pop artist, Andy Warhol. Not only this, we investigate the lives of the assassins, would-be or successful: the 'nobodies' whose lives show how a combination of personality flaws and social deprivation work together to create a fanatic.

Find out about all this as we lead you through the dramatic stories of assassinations – both successful and failed – that aimed to change the course of world history.

CHAPTER ONE

PRIME TARGETS

Prime ministers and presidents of the world's nations are, of course, an obvious target for assassination. In any country at any time, the leader of the nation is perhaps the most high profile, well-known face in the press and on TV. He or she is also one of the most powerful individuals in the country. No wonder that, around the world, most assassins choose these leaders as their prime target.

In Asia, the assassination of South Korean President Park Chung Hee during a shoot-out at a secret political meeting was one of the most dramatic, violent murders of a political leader ever to hit the headlines; while in Africa, the shameful execution of the first prime minister of the Congo, Patrice Lumumba, by a firing squad in the bush, as he tried to escape with his life, was an equally compelling, dramatic scenario. In Europe, the killing of Swedish Prime Minister Olof Palme as he walked quietly through the streets of Stockholm with his wife after a trip to the cinema, was drama of a different kind. His death marked a sad end to the traditional liberalism and tolerance of the Swedish nation: the first time in centuries, the peace-loving, democratic way of life of one of Europe's most socially progressive countries had been shattered.

In some cases, political leaders have appeared to be a target because of their extreme ideological views and actions: for example, Hendrik Verwoerd, the South African prime minister and architect of apartheid during the early part of the twentieth century. Yet, surprisingly, Verwoerd's killing did not appear to be the result of any conspiracy or political plot, but the action of a mentally unbalanced loner, albeit a person of mixed race who had first-hand experience of the divisive nature of apartheid.

In other cases, leaders have been assassinated as a result of a conspiracy: for example the Egyptian President Anwar Sadat; however, lack of support for the conspirators' cause – in this case, to replace the secular government with a Muslim one – led to the eventual failure of the plan to take over power.

As well as these assassinations, there are a handful that caused profound shock around the entire globe, and arguably changed the course of world history. The assassination of Mahatma Gandhi, the Indian premier, in 1948 seemed to spell the end of an era of new hope and optimism that Hindus and Muslims on the Asian subcontinent could live together in peace and harmony. Likewise, the assassination of John F. Kennedy in 1963 seemed to close a chapter in America's history when, for a while, it was hoped that black and white people could coexist in justice and equality, after the bitter years of oppression, poverty and racism endured by Afro-Americans throughout the United States since the days of slavery.

Throughout history, the premiers of the world's nations have had to walk a dangerous line, trying to balance the opposing interests of different political, ethnic, religious and other factions within their countries. They have not always succeeded; indeed, in some cases, they have faced an impossible task. Most of them have had to live with the constant threat of assassination, and most have survived. These are the stories of those who did not.

Gandhi led civil disobedience in India. Here, he marches to the shore at Dandi to collect salt in defiance of the law

MAHATMA GANDHI

Mohandas Karamchad Gandhi has a permanent place in history as one of the greatest leaders of the twentieth century. His aim was to seek independence for his country, India, from its British colonial rulers through a campaign of non-violence. During his lifetime, he set an example to his people by pursuing a highly principled, moral way of life, dressing in the clothes of an Indian peasant and eschewing the trappings of luxury. As well as advocating non-violence, Gandhi also believed that people of all religious persuasions should have equal rights, and that Hindus were no more important than Muslims, which made him many enemies among radical Hindu political factions in India. On 30 January 1948, Gandhi was assassinated at the hands of a Hindu fanatic, Nathuram Godse, who shot and killed him as he walked through the streets to attend a prayer meeting in New Delhi. At his funeral, the nation mourned the loss of the man they called 'Mahatma', or 'great soul', and the prime minister of the newly independent India announced, 'the light has gone out of our lives'.

Non-violent protest

Born in 1869 in Porbander, western India, Gandhi travelled to London, England, as a young man and studied law there. He began his career as a lawyer in Bombay, but soon moved to South Africa, where he took part in non-violent protests against the government, in support of Indian immigrants' rights there. On his return to India in 1915, he

Gandhi at 10 Downing Street. He dressed like a simple peasant, jogging the world's memory about India's terrible poverty

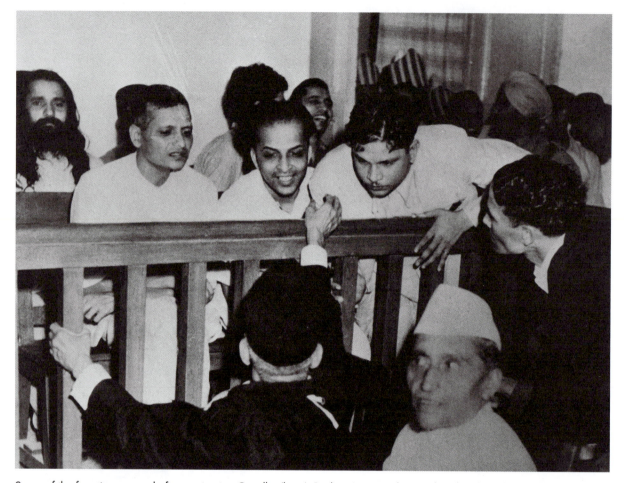

Some of the fanatics accused of assassinating Gandhi: (l to r) Godse, Apte, Krishna and Badge (bearded in the second row)

became involved in politics, and began to campaign on behalf of the Indian National Congress against the British government, encouraging Indians to buy Indian rather than British goods. He consistently advocated non-violent protest, but even so, he was imprisoned several times for his activities. He became a thorn in the side of the British authorities, showing up their hypocritical attitudes, and attracting attention wherever he went. In 1931, he famously attended a political conference in Britain dressed only in the simple clothes of an Indian peasant, once again reminding the world of the harsh poverty in which many of his countrymen lived.

After many years of political campaigning, Gandhi began to see his dream of a free, independent India become a reality, with the break-up of British colonial rule. However, there were other problems on the horizon that threatened to destroy the country's peaceful transition to independence, in particular the deep antagonism that existed between Indian Hindus and Muslims. Having co-operated with the British, Gandhi was accused of helping to partition the country, a step that by all accounts he fundamentally opposed. He was also criticized for weakening the Hindus' political power through his belief in the equality of all religious faiths.

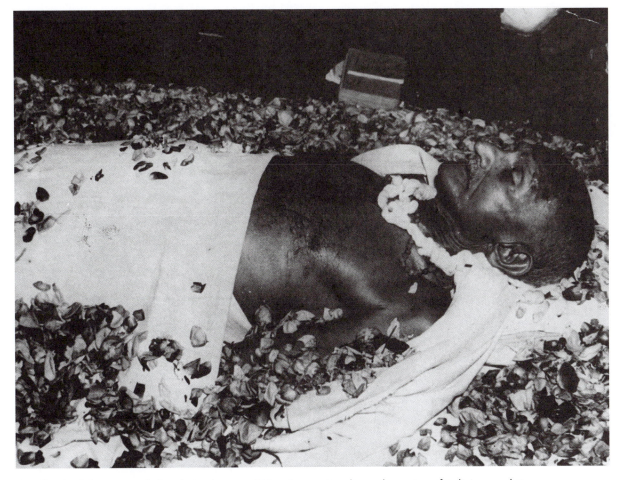

Gandhi's body lay in state before being burnt and his ashes scattered over the waters of India's sacred rivers

Despite the criticisms, Gandhi continued to be regarded by the majority of the Indian people as the father of Indian independence, and as such became, by the end of his life, one of the most famous, well-loved figures in the country.

Assassination attempts

On 20 January 1948, there was an assassination attempt on Gandhi, but it failed. Ten days later, an assassin struck again, and this time was successful. Gandhi was on his way to a prayer meeting at Birla House, the home of a prominent industrialist where he often stayed during his visits to New Delhi. At about five o'clock, people began to gather for the meeting. According to witnesses, Gandhi arrived for the meeting at about twelve minutes past five, dressed in his usual garb, though wearing a homespun shawl over his loin cloth, because it was a cold evening. As he walked across the grass, accompanied by various followers, including some young women, onlookers knelt down or bowed their heads before him. Then, suddenly, several shots rang out. Gandhi fell to the ground, mortally wounded, his loin cloth heavily stained with blood. A doctor rushed to the scene, but it was too late to save the victim. As Gandhi lay dying, the police took charge, dispersing the weeping crowds and carrying the body away.

At 6 p.m. on All India Radio, it was announced that a lone gunman had shot Gandhi on his way to Birla House. He had been killed by three pistol shots in his chest. The killer was Nathuram Godse, a Hindu activitist who was thought to be connected to the Hindu organization Mahasabha. Godse was immediately taken into custody and was tried and convicted. He received a death sentence and was hanged on 15 November 1949. Four other conspirators, including Godse's brother Gopal, were given life sentences. The president of the Mahasabha, Vinayak Damodar Savarkar, was also thought to be behind the assassination, but there was not enough evidence to link him to it.

Gandhi's last words

Not surprisingly, given the confusion of the assassination events, accounts differ as to what Gandhi actually said as he lay dying. Some attest that his last words were 'He Ram!' (Oh God!), which may have expressed his spiritual commitment to God, or – as some commentators have pointed out – could just be the normal expression of surprise and shock on being attacked. Whatever the truth, these are the words that are inscribed on Gandhi's memorial tomb in New Delhi. Others believe that the Mahatma exclaimed 'Rama Rama' and that as he fell, he put his hands together in the gesture of 'namaste', a religious gesture symbolizing love, respect and connection to others.

After his death, Gandhi was cremated on a funeral pyre as is the Hindu custom, and his ashes collected in twenty urns. These were taken around India, and the ashes scattered among the waters of the country's great rivers, in accordance with Gandhi's wishes.

Today, Gandhi is remembered in India as the architect of independence, and his philosophy of non-violence and civil disobedience is thought to have inspired freedom fighters around the world, including Martin Luther King, the Dalai Lama, Nelson Mandela, Steve Biko, and Aung San Suu Kyi. But according to Gandhi himself, his teachings were nothing new: as he often stated, 'Truth and non-violence are as old as the hills.'

ABRAHAM LINCOLN

The assassination of Abraham Lincoln on 14 April 1865 is, arguably, the first modern political assassination.

This was not an especially mysterious crime. Abraham Lincoln had led the Union side throughout the extraordinarily bitter and bloody conflict known as the American Civil War (or the War Between The States, if you're a southerner). At the time of his death the Union forces had finally prevailed. Not only that, but during the course of the war Lincoln had proclaimed emancipation, freeing the slaves in those southern states that the northern Union forces occupied.

As a result, there were many who wanted Lincoln dead: supporters of the southern Confederacy in general and pro-slavers in particular. One such man was the actor John Wilkes Booth, born on 10 May 1838. Booth had achieved some success on the stage, including landing several parts in Shakespeare plays. As a confirmed racist

Abraham Lincoln led the Union side throughout the American Civil War and was a staunch defender of emancipation

On 14 April 1865, John Wilkes Booth shot Abraham Lincoln in the head at near point-blank range with a single-shot derringer

and southern sympathizer, he loathed Abraham Lincoln.

In the late summer of 1864 it was becoming clear that the Union forces were winning the war. Booth's original plan (whether devised by himself alone, or in collaboration with more senior Confederate figures) was to kidnap Lincoln, take him to Richmond, the Confederate capital, and hold him in return

for Confederate prisoners of war. By January 1865, Booth had organized a group of helpers that included Samuel Arnold, Michael O'Laughlen, John Surratt, Lewis Powell, George Atzerodt, and David Herold. He used a boarding house belonging to Mary Surratt to meet with his co-conspirators.

The kidnap was due to take place on 17 March 1865, when Lincoln was scheduled to attend a play at a hospital near Washington. However, the president changed his plans at the last moment and the plot failed. Before it could be re-arranged, General Robert E. Lee surrendered to General Ulysses S. Grant at Appomattox on 9 April 1865, effectively ending the Civil War. Two days later, Booth was present as Lincoln made a speech in Washington suggesting that voting rights be granted to certain blacks. Booth decided it was time for yet more desperate action.

With his comrades, Booth came up with an ambitious plot to assassinate not just Lincoln but also the vice president and the secretary of state. Booth wanted to be the one to actually shoot Lincoln. The aim was to kill the president and to cause chaos, so that the Confederates would have one last chance to strike back.

On the morning of Friday 14 April, Booth visited Ford's Theater and was delighted to discover that the perfect opportunity was about to be presented to him. The president was planning to attend the theatre that very evening to watch a play called *Our American Cousin*. Booth held one final meeting with his co-conspirators. He would shoot Lincoln at the theatre; Atzerodt was to shoot Vice-President Andrew Johnson; and Powell was given the job of shooting Secretary of State William Seward. Herold would accompany Powell. All three attacks were planned for 10.15 p.m. that night.

The president arrived at the theatre at about 8.30 p.m. An hour later Booth arrived, carrying a single shot derringer and a hunting knife. Booth gave his horse to a boy who held it for him in the rear alley, while he went to the saloon next door for a little Dutch

courage. Around 10.07 p.m. he came back into the theatre, and gradually made his way toward the state box where the Lincolns were sitting. Lincoln's personal bodyguard, meanwhile, had left his post. At about 10.15 p.m., Booth opened the door to the state box and shot Lincoln in the back of the head at near point-blank range. As chaos broke out, one of Lincoln's companions, Henry Rathbone, tried to restrain Booth. Booth stabbed Rathbone in the arm and jumped some eleven feet to the stage below, breaking his leg as he landed. He dragged himself to his feet, shouted 'Sic Semper Tyrannis' (Latin for 'As Always to Tyrants', and the Virginia state motto) and hobbled off the stage before any of the shocked audience could stop him. Booth went out of the back door, climbed on his horse, and escaped from the city using the Navy Yard Bridge.

His cohorts were less successful. Atzerodt never even tried to kill Johnson, and Powell stabbed Seward but failed to kill him. At around midnight Booth reached Mary Surratt's tavern in Surrattsville where he met David Herold, before heading off to a sympathetic doctor who set and splinted Booth's broken leg.

Back in Washington, Lincoln never regained consciousness and finally died at 7.22 a.m. the next morning. Booth and Herold remained at large for another eleven days before the Federal authorities caught up with them and found them hiding in a barn near Port Royal, Virginia, early in the morning of 26 April. Herold surrendered but Booth refused, so the forces set the barn on fire. Booth was eventually shot dead by Sergeant Boston Corbett.

Within days, Booth's co-conspirators were arrested by the government. They were tried by a military tribunal, and all were found guilty. Powell, Atzerodt, Herold and Mrs Surratt were all hanged on 7 July 1865.

That was the effective end of the story. The assassin and his henchmen had been found and dealt with. However, speculation has raged ever since that there may have been a wider conspiracy behind the assassination. Some suggest that the vice president himself might have been behind it; others point the finger at the secretary of war. Others still have suggested such unlikely culprits as the Vatican or international bankers. Rather more plausible, though, is the idea that Booth's operation may have been directed by more senior Confederate leaders, in particular Judah Benjamin, the Confederate secretary of state. Today, many modern historians support this view.

JOHN F. KENNEDY

The assassination of John F. Kennedy on 22 November 1963 was one of the most significant events of the twentieth century. Not only the dramatic shooting itself, but the very public nature of the killing, which was widely televised, made it one of the pivotal moments of the century. The killing took place when Kennedy paid an official visit to the city of Dallas, Texas, at 12.30 p.m. as he was riding through Dealey Plaza in a motorcade, waving to the thronging crowds. For many, it marked a sudden, tragic end to a period of optimism in America, in which civil rights campaigns were flourishing and

there seemed to be new hope for a better future. In retrospect, this faith in the prospect of change and progress seems perhaps to have been naïve; but whatever the reality, the assassination of the youthful president, who seemed to embody these ideals, was a profound blow to the nation's new-found confidence in its ability to create a more just, peaceful and egalitarian society.

Shot in the head

The run-up to that fateful day had been a tense one. The president wanted to visit Dallas as part of his re-election campaign, and to raise funds for the Democratic party, but there had been a number of rowdy protests against political figures who had appeared in public in the previous months. The president's security men were also concerned that the motorcade might be a target for a gunman who could hide in the crowd or in a nearby building. However, on the day, all seemed to go smoothly at first, and the motorcade had nearly completed its route by the time the incident occurred.

Just before 12.30 p.m. the car passed the Texas School Book Depository, from where a number of shots were fired at the president's limousine. Strangely, while this was happening, the limousine slowed down. The president was mortally wounded, struck in the shoulder and then by a bullet in the head, while the governor of Texas, John Connally, was also shot and seriously injured.

A security man jumped on to the car to shield the president and his wife, but by then it was too late. Kennedy and Governor Connally lay bleeding as the car sped off to

John F. Kennedy and his wife Jackie enjoy the drive through Dallas in their motorcade. Moments later the president was shot

the nearest hospital, Parkland Memorial, with their wives doing the best they could to keep them alive until they got there. During the tragedy, many of the people in the crowd were unaware that anything was amiss, thinking that the bullet sounds had just been the backfiring of a car.

Unprofessional autopsy

When the president arrived at the hospital, it was clear to staff that he was not going to survive. A priest was called, but by the time he arrived, the president had died. Meanwhile, Governor Connally was undergoing emergency surgery, and

eventually pulled through. His wife's action of pulling him on to her lap in the car, so that the wound in his chest was able to close up, had helped to save his life. Had she not done so, he would almost certainly have bled to death.

That afternoon, Kennedy's body was taken from the hospital and driven over to the presidential aeroplane. This was against regulations, and was to cause concern in the investigation that took place after the event. Since this was a murder, there should have been a forensic examination by the coroner before the body left the hospital; however, this was never done. The Presidential aeroplane flew the body to Washington DC, where an autopsy was performed at Bethesda Naval Hospital. Unfortunately, the autopsy was done in a thoroughly unprofessional manner, so that important information about what exactly killed the president, and the manner in which he died, was not recorded properly.

Lone gunman?

Confusion also reigned when the death of the president was announced publicly. Many Americans were shocked and frightened, thinking perhaps it was part of a Soviet attack on the United States.

Traffic came to a halt in many areas, and children were sent home early from school. TV and radio stations stopped their usual broadcasts, and for the next few days there was non-stop reporting on the assassination and its aftermath. When they heard the news, people cried and hugged each other in the streets, not only in America, but across the world. On the day of Kennedy's funeral, the 25 November, a national day of mourning was declared, and thousands thronged to see the president's coffin. At the funeral, heads of state from over ninety countries were present.

A week after the assassination, an inquiry known as The Warren Commission was set up to find out exactly what had happened. However, despite its efforts, it failed to account for the many puzzling aspects of the murder. The Commission found that a lone gunman, Lee Harvey Oswald, had fired three shots at the president: the first had missed the motorcade; the second had wounded both Kennedy and the governor of Texas; and

a last shot had hit Kennedy in the head. This final shot had killed the president. These theories became known as the 'lone gunman theory' and the 'single bullet theory' (often jokingly referred to as the 'Magic Bullet Theory' because it seemed so unlikely that the same bullet would hit two people). In time, the theories were questioned – not only by experts, but by the American public in general, who were often polled about the matter.

History of mental disturbance

It turned out that the assassin, Lee Harvey Oswald, had a history of mental illness, and also had links to the Soviet Union. He had been born in New Orleans on 18 October 1939. His father had died shortly after his birth, and at the age of three, his mother had sent him to live in a children's home. Later, when his mother remarried, he rejoined his family, but as a teenager, he showed behaviour problems.

As a young man, he became a Marxist and joined the US Marines, where he served abroad. He subsequently left the Marines, and visited the Soviet Union, where he applied to become a citizen. When his request was rejected by the authorities, he attempted suicide, and was then allowed to stay in the country. He married, had a child, and then moved back to the US.

His wife later claimed that in 1963, he had attempted to assassinate General Edwin Walker, a right-wing political figure. When Oswald moved to Dallas, and found work in the Texas School Book Depository, he planned his next killing.

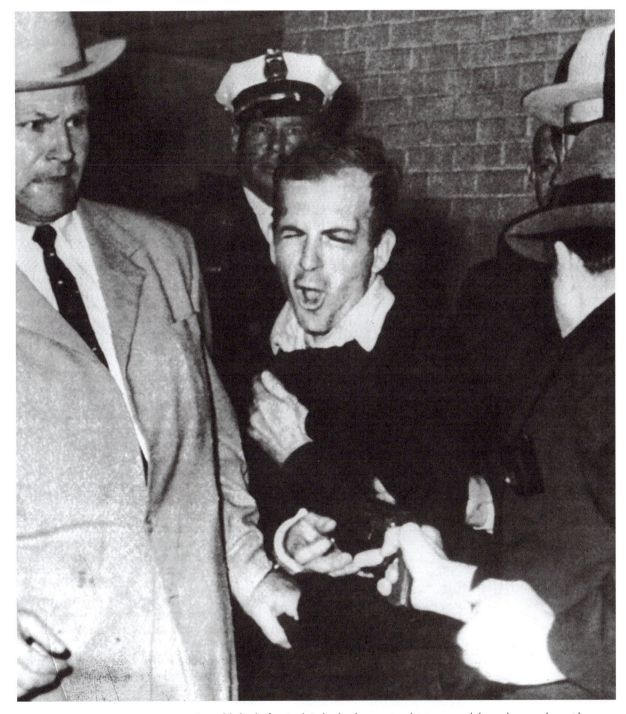

Lone assassin or patsy? Lee Harvey Oswald died after Jack Ruby had mysteriously penetrated the police cordon with a gun

On the day of the assassination, Oswald was seen at his workplace at 11.55am, and then again at 12.31pm. His landlady later testified that he had come home after that, followed by a police car. He had then gone out, and had been approached in the street by a police officer, J.D. Tippet.

At this point, he pulled out a gun and fired at the police officer several times before running away, leaving the policeman dying on the street.

Helped by members of the public, other

Jack Ruby with a couple of his dancers outside the Carousel Club: Ruby shot Lee Harvey Oswald two days after his arrest

officers managed to pursue Oswald and he was soon under arrrest.

Once in police custody, Oswald revealed where he worked, and the police soon realized that he had had ample opportunity to shoot the president from a location in the building. They also found that his hand print matched a print on the rifle found near the scene of the crime. Moreover, witnesses testified that they had actually seen Oswald shooting from the window. Further investigation showed that he had bought the rifle under an assumed name.

Assassin assassinated

To add to the confusion, on 24 November 1963 Jack Ruby, a Dallas nightclub owner, shot Oswald in the stomach from point-blank range, while he was in police custody. Oswald died soon afterwards. Once again, the murder took place in full view of the public, and once again it prompted a new wave of speculation: how was it that Ruby had found it so easy to penetrate the security surrounding Oswald? Had he killed Oswald to prevent him from telling the truth about who was really behind the killing? Was the assassination planned by the Soviet government, or perhaps even by the Mafia?

Jacob Rubenstein, also known as Jack Ruby, was known to have links to organized crime. The fifth of eight children, he had been born to Polish immigrants in Chicago. His father had been a violent man, and his mother had suffered from mental illness. He had been brought up in a foster home. As a young man, he had worked in a number of jobs before being called up to the air force, and at the end of the war had begun to run night clubs in Dallas. Between 1949 and November 24 1963, Ruby was arrested eight times by the Dallas Police Department on charges which included disturbing the peace, carrying a concealed weapon and permitting dancing after hours. He was also frequently suspended by the Texas Liquor Control Board.

At first, Ruby claimed that he had shot Oswald out of sympathy for Kennedy's widow, but he then changed his plea to insanity. He was, however, convicted of the murder and sentenced to death. Later, his conviction was overturned, but he died from cancer on 3 January 1967 while awaiting a new trial.

The mystery remains

In 1976, a House Select Committee re-examined the evidence surrounding the president's assassination and the killing of Lee Harvey Oswald. The committee now found that there were possibly two gunmen, and that the final bullet had not been fired by Oswald, but from an unknown gunman hiding in an area known as the Grassy Knoll. Evidence was also collected from eye witnesses and from people who had photographed, filmed or recorded the event. However, the report was inconclusive: it merely suggested that, given the probability of there being two gunmen responsible (a theory based on acoustic recordings of the gunshots fired), a conspiracy of some kind seemed likely. To this day, although there are plenty of lurid theories as to who was behind the assassination of John F. Kennedy, no absolutely conclusive account as to what really happened on that fateful day has yet been advanced.

PATRICE LUMUMBA

Patrice Lumumba became the prime minister of the newly independent Republic of the Congo in 1960. From the start, his tenure was an unstable one. Although independence had been declared, in reality the Belgian government had not given up its interests in the Congo, and there were still many Belgians left in the country, who had support from Africans there. The new prime minister, who was well known as a radical and a firebrand, was viewed with extreme suspicion from the start.

There were rebellions against the newly elected government, and after only a few months, it dissolved into chaos. Lumumba was forced to leave office. He went on the run, fearing for his life, but was assassinated by Belgian forces on 17 January 1961. The fact that his ignominious murder went unpunished at the time showed just how little the Belgians, and the West in general, had genuinely ceded power to the Africans, and was a clear indication that independence could not be achieved by peaceful means, as had been promised.

'Tears, fire, and blood'

Patrice Emery Lumumba was born on 2 July 1925 in Onalua, which at the time was part of the Belgian Congo. He attended a missionary school and later became a journalist. A highly intelligent man, he soon became interested in politics, and began to work for a trade union. He also joined the Belgian Liberal party, but was arrested and charged with embezzling funds. He remained in prison for a year, which helped to radicalize him, and on his release became a founding member of the MNC, the National Congolese Movement. During this time, the Belgian government promised to release the Congo from the empire within five years. In local elections, the MNC did well, and the date for independence was brought forward from 1964 to 1960. After the national elections, Lumumba became prime minister of the new Democratic Republic of the Congo, with Joseph Kasavubu as his president.

It was clear that Lumumba's task was not going to be an easy one. In the ceremony marking the transition of the country to an independent state, the King of Belgium gave a speech praising the great achievements of the Belgian monarchy and the Belgian people in civilizing the Congo. He talked of how the Belgians had liberated the Congolese from the slave trade, how they had modernized the country, and commented on how inexperienced the Africans were at governing themselves. Lumumba was incensed, and delivered a speech in which he remembered the 'tears, fire, and blood' that characterized the struggle of the Congolese people to free themselves from the yoke of poverty and oppression imposed on them by the colonial regime. He recalled the true history of his country, in which black people were forced to live in miserable conditions, treated as inferiors by their white masters, and forced to yield their lands and their wealth to their colonial overlords. He pointed to the fact that those blacks who had dared to protest had been exiled from their country, or shot

Attempting to flee to his stronghold at Stanleyville, Patrice Lemumba was seized by hostile troops and returned to Leopoldville

Moise Tshombe declared Katanga independent of the new republic and seems later to have ordered the killing of Lumumba

in cold blood by the authorities. He proclaimed that those days were now over, and that the Congo was now in the hands of its own people. He called on its citizens to begin a new struggle, to build a strong country where black people were equal and free, so that the Congolese could be an inspiration to the rest of Africa.

Decapitation threats

Not surprisingly, the Belgians were not best pleased with Lumumba's speech, and within weeks of his taking office, trouble began. The first sign of it was an uprising in the province of Katanga, which declared itself independent from the new republic. The protest was led by Moise Tshombe, with the support of the Belgian government. Lumumba was forced to seek aid from the Soviet Union to restore order in the province. The president, Kasavubu, then dismissed Lumumba from office, which many considered an illegal act, since the president was only supposed to have ceremonial, rather than actual, powers. Lumumba refused to go, and tried to dismiss Kasavubu from office. Kasavubu had the support of sections of the military, who now staged a coup, led by Colonel Joseph Mobutu. (Mobutu later became infamous as the tyrannical president of the Congo, with a regime that lasted for thirty-five years.) Mobutu in turn was supported by the Belgians and the CIA, who were working in the country to prevent the radical Lumumba from remaining in office.

Lumumba's life was now in danger, and he had no choice but to abandon his post. On 1 December 1961, he fled to Stanleyville, and on the way was captured by Mobutu's men and charged with inciting the army to rebellion. At this point, the United Nations intervened, asking that Lumumba be properly treated according to the laws of the land. The Soviet Union demanded that the UN restore Lumumba to power as prime minister, and asked for Mobutu to be disarmed. Lumumba's supporters then began to threaten that, unless he was released immediately, there would be violence, including decapitation, against all Belgians still living in the Congo. The tension escalated as the Soviet Union refused to permit the UN increased powers to deal with the situation, and several countries began to withdraw their forces from the UN army there.

Beaten and abused

Amid rumours that he was being mistreated by his captors, Lumumba was transferred to a prison in the Katanga province, where he was extremely unpopular.

There were stories that he and several of his aides had been beaten by policemen there. Eventually, it was decided that Lumumba should be dismissed from his post but allowed to return to his official residence, where he was placed under house arrest.

Lumumba then escaped, leaving the house quietly at night in a visitor's car. However, it was not long before Mobutu's troops caught up with him, capturing him once more. Lumumba appealed to the UN to intervene, but the local officers refused to help, saying that since he had evaded UN protection, he would now have to fend for himself.

After the killing, Patrice Lumumba's brother Louis came to Leopoldville though it wasn't clear whether he was free or under guard

Mobutu's men then took him to Mobutu's residence, where he was publicly humiliated and beaten in front of the world's media. Lumumba was then put into the custody of his enemy Tshombe, the leader of the Katangan uprising, who it seems may have ordered his killing.

A firing squad

There is some controversy as to who was behind Lumumba's assassination, but whoever it was, there is little doubt that Patrice Lumumba was murdered by Katangan soldiers, commanded by Belgian officers. What appears to have happened is that Lumumba was led into the bush, where an army firing squad was waiting for him. Lumumba and two of his government aides were lined up and shot, one at a time, in front of Tshombe and other officials. The bodies were buried, and later dissolved in acid to cover up the deaths. Some of Lumumba's teeth, and a piece of his skull, were kept as macabre mementoes.

It was a while before news of the assassination leaked out. The official story was that Lumumba had escaped from custody and been murdered by hostile villagers. However, many years later, documentation was unearthed showing that Belgian soldiers had been present at his assassination. In 2002, the Belgian government issued a statement admitting 'partial' responsibility for Lumumba's murder, and apologizing to the Congolese people.

Later, it was also revealed that during the 1960s, President Eisenhower had called on the CIA to murder Lumumba during a meeting with high-ranking officials, as Lumumba was considered a Communist threat to Western security. However, there is no evidence to show that the CIA was directly involved in the assassination – though some believe that the CIA did, in fact, plot to murder Lumumba, but were beaten to it by the Belgians and the Katangans. Whoever was immediately responsible, it remains clear that the assassination of Patrice Lumumba, the first democratically elected prime minister of the Congo, was a deeply shameful incident in the republic's history.

ANWAR SADAT

The assassination of Anwar Sadat on 6 October 1981 brought to a dramatic close the life of one of Egypt's most important and controversial leaders. As the third president of Egypt, he served for over a decade, from 1970 until 1981, and worked to restore peace between Israel and the Arab nations, for which he was awarded the Nobel Prize. However, his policies caused a great deal of anger from fundamentalist Arabs and others, who saw his efforts to mend relations with Israel as entirely motivated by a desire to make Egypt stronger economically, at the expense of the other Arab peoples, particularly the Palestinians. His eventual assassination was masterminded by a fundamentalist group, one of whom was to be involved, many years later, in the bombing of the World Trade Center in 1993.

Sadat was born to a large family in Mit Abu Al-Kum, Al-Minufiyah, forty miles north of Cairo, in 1918. He had twelve brothers and sisters. His parents were of Sudanese and Egyptian descent. His father worked as a clerk in the local military hospital. Sadat grew up at a time when Egypt was effectively a British colony, and was aware of the poverty that the country had been thrown into as a result. One of the most troubling aspects of British rule for the Egyptians was that the British and French had control over the country's most valuable asset, the Suez Canal, which linked the Mediterranean to the Indian Ocean. Egypt had been forced, by debt, to relinquish its interests in the canal, and as a result, could make no profit from it.

As a young man, Sadat's experiences convinced him the British hold over Egypt was unjust. For example, a man named Zahran, who came from a small village like his own, was hanged for taking part in a protest in which a British officer had been killed. His courage as he made his way through the streets to his death impressed the young Sadat enormously. Sadat was also interested in politics, and learned about the lives of great statesmen such as Kemal Atatürk of Turkey, who had defeated the Ottoman Empire and liberated his people, as well as making reforms and modernizing the country. Sadat also admired Mahatma Gandhi, who had toured Egypt in 1932, and had given speeches extolling the virtues of non-violent action and civil disobedience as a way of achieving liberation. Unfortunately, Sadat also admired Adolf Hitler, whom he saw as a potential threat to British colonial rule in Egypt and elsewhere around the world.

A bright student, Sadat enrolled in the British-run Royal Military Academy in Cairo, where he studied military tactics. He graduated as a signals officer, and was posted to a remote area of the country, where he met a number of other men whose politics were similar to his own, including Colonel Gamal Abdel Nasser, the future leader of Egypt.

Sadat, Nasser and a group of other young officers formed the Free Officers Movement, a clandestine organization dedicated to the overthrow of the Egyptian monarchy and its British advisors.

As a result of his revolutionary activities, which included seeking support from the Nazis during the Second World War, Sadat was imprisoned twice. During his days in jail, he taught himself English and French. When he was released, he left the army for a while and involved himself in business, through which he met 16-year-old Jehan Raouf. He divorced his wife Ehsan Madi to marry Jehan, and the couple went on to have three children.

In 1952, members of the Free Officers Movement mounted a successful coup, paving the way for Arab nationalists in other countries – especially in Libya, Syria and Saudi Arabia. The Egyptian monarchy was ousted, and with it the British colonialists. At the head of the new government was Nasser, who appointed Sadat as his public relations minister. One of Sadat's first tasks was to present the abdication of King Farouk to the public in a positive light, through the media network.

Four years later, Nasser nationalized the Suez Canal, much to the fury of the British and French, who now stood to lose their considerable economic interest in the

Anwar Sadat was taking the salute at a military parade in Cairo when Islamic Jihad operatives opened fire on him

In November 1979, Sadat (second right) raised his nation's flag at St Catherine's Monastery, Mount Sinai, on land handed back to Egypt by Israel

shipping link. In conjunction with the newly established, anti-Arab state of Israel, the British and the French declared war on Egypt, but the Egyptians retained control of the canal, and eventually the British retreated, under pressure from the United States. Egypt went on to build itself up as a new nation, under the leadership of Nasser and his right-hand man Sadat, maintaining a profile of being independent and unaligned, while becoming a shining example to those colonized countries who desired independence.

During this time, Sadat held many positions of prominence in the government, becoming vice president, minister of state, and secretary to the National Union. When Nasser died in 1970, Sadat took over the presidency, in the process getting rid of his opponents in what was termed, by the state-owned media, 'the corrective revolution'.

Sadat's experience in the early days of Egypt's independence had led him to make pragmatic alliances, in order to preserve and augment his own country's political and economic strength. In previous times, there

A wounded man is tended to in the grandstand as all around is chaos in the bloody aftermath of Sadat's assassination

The scattered chairs in the grandstand showed the panic caused by the murderous attack of Islamic Jihad gunmen

had been constant animosity between Israel and Egypt, and bouts of warfare had seriously damaged the Egyptian economy. However, Sadat now attempted to build a peace settlement between the Egyptians and the Israelis. He became the first Arab leader to do so, and in 1978, negotiated the Camp David Accords with Israeli Prime Minister Menachem Begin. The following year, Sadat and Begin received the Nobel Peace Prize for their efforts. However, there were those who felt that the move was a disastrous one, ignoring the needs of the Palestinians and betraying Egypt's role as independent leader of the Arab peoples. In the view of many Muslims, Sadat had 'sold out' to the Israelis purely to benefit Egypt, forgetting the plight of Arabs across the world.

Despite the major advantages Sadat gained from the Peace Accords – for example, the

Israelis handed back large territories to Egypt – he became extremely unpopular in his own country. One of the reasons for this was that he had begun to suppress dissident voices to his regime, arresting hundreds of members of Muslim and Coptic organizations, in an entirely illiberal and unjust way. It was not long before a fatwa was issued against him, by Omar Abdel-Rahman, an imam who was later convicted for his role in the bombing of the World Trade Center in 1993.

The treaty with Egypt had led to peace but not prosperity and the president's popularity plummeted. As Sadat turned the screw on his opponents, he also imposed a series of referendums over his policies upon the Egyptians which he kept winning with more than ninety-nine per cent of the vote. No one was convinced. In July 1981, there was religious violence in poor parts of Cairo and men, women and children were slaughtered. Tensions were growing.

On 6 October 1981, Sadat attended a parade in Cairo. While he was there, a group of soldiers, who were members of the Egyptian Islamic Jihad, managed to penetrate the tight security around Sadat. They parked an army truck full of soldiers right next to the stand where the president was inspecting the troops, and a lieutenant walked up to him. Sadat waited for the man to salute him, but as he did, the soldiers stood up in the truck, and fired a round of bullets at the president. They also threw grenades at him for good measure. Then Khalid Islambouli, the leader of the group, ran towards the president, shouting 'Death to the Pharaoh!' and firing at him.

As Sadat fell to the ground, his security guards opened fire on the assassins. In the shoot-out that followed, seven onlookers were killed, and twenty-eight wounded. One of those that died was the ambassador for Cuba, and a Greek Orthodox priest. Among the wounded was Sadat's successor, Hosni Mubarak, whose hand was injured. Immediately the fight was over, Sadat was rushed to hospital, but he died shortly afterwards.

The leader of the assassin group turned out to be Khalid Ahmed Showky El-Islambouli, a soldier who had graduated from the Military Academy with distinction. His brother Mohamed was also arrested, and found to be a member of a religious fundamentalist group who had ordered the murder. Khalid was standing in that day at the parade for another soldier who had been unable to attend because he was praying at Mecca.

Khalid El-Islambouli was brought to trial and charged with the murder of the president, Anwar Sadat. He was convicted of the crime, and was sentenced to death. In April 1982, he was executed.

After Sadat's killing, in a move that shocked the Egyptians, the Iranians named a street in Teheran after Islambouli. However, there were many nations around the world that mourned the death of the president, and his funeral was attended by a record number of international dignitaries, including four presidents of the United States: Ronald Reagan, and former presidents, Gerald Ford, Jimmy Carter and Richard Nixon. Also present was Boutros Boutros-Ghali, who was later to become head of the United Nations.

OLOF PALME

Sweden is traditionally a country where law and order prevails, and where well-known figures from the world of politics and showbusiness are at liberty to walk the streets without bodyguards and other security measures. However, this perception of a law-abiding country where tolerance and non-violence is the rule came to a swift end on 28 February 1986, when Prime Minister Olof Palme was shot dead in cold blood on the streets of Stockholm, on his way back from a trip to the cinema with his wife. To this day, the assassin has not been found, and there are conflicting theories as to who committed the crime. As a result, a number of conspiracy theories about Olof Palme's death have grown up, and political commentators continue to puzzle over what really happened to one of Sweden's most famous international statesmen of all time.

Political radical

Olof Palme was born in Ostermalm, Stockholm, Sweden, on 30 January 1927. He came from a politically conservative, upper-class family. As a young man, he studied at the University of Stockholm, and joined the Social Democratic Party (SAP). He came to the attention of Swedish political leaders when he became President of the United Students Union. In this capacity, he travelled around the third world, witnessing extreme poverty at first hand. He also studied in the United States, and was taken aback by the racism he saw there. Both these experiences were to mould his future politics, and he

became committed to a radical programme of equality, democracy and a fairer economic system for all, not only in Sweden, but throughout the world.

On completing his studies, Palme went on to work for Tage Erlander, then the prime minister of Sweden. His rise in politics was swift, and by 1955, he had become leader of the youth section of the Social Democratic Labour Party. In the years that followed, Palme became one of the most influential figures in the party, holding many important government posts, including minister for education and cultural affairs, and minister for communications. In 1969, he reached the top of his career ladder, becoming prime minister of Sweden.

As prime minister, he carried out several radical constitutional reforms, but his popularity waned when he introduced plans to increase taxation so as to fund an expanding welfare programme in Sweden. He was voted out of office, but then continued his career internationally, working for the United Nations and trying to achieve a solution to the war between Iraq and Iran. This proved impossible, but in the process he became an internationally respected statesman.

Shot twice in the stomach

In 1982, Palme was voted back into power, and continued to work as before on a programme of social democratic reforms. Four years later, on 28 February 1986, he was walking home from the cinema one evening with his wife, Lisbet. Despite his fame, he did not surround himself with bodyguards, as is the custom for political

Olof Palme outlines his plans for an alliance of neutral countries to balance the Superpowers – the US and the Soviet Union

leaders and celebrities in many countries, but walked freely around the streets at all times of day and night, so much so that he had become a familiar face in central Stockholm. In Sweden, this kind of freedom was taken for granted, since street violence was comparatively rare. However, that fateful evening, his confidence in the civilized, law-abiding nature of his countrymen and women proved misplaced.

Olof Palme and his wife Lisbet left the cinema at about half past eleven. As they walked down the quiet streets, they were ambushed by a gunman, who shot the prime minister twice in the stomach. His wife was shot in the back and wounded. A passing taxi driver rushed to help the couple, calling the emergency services on his mobile radio. In addition, two young girls who were sitting in a car close to where the shooting happened ran out to help the injured pair while they were waiting for an ambulance to arrive. The ambulance then sped through the streets to the nearest hospital, but it was too late to save Palme – when he arrived at the hospital he was pronounced dead. His wife was treated for her injury and survived the ordeal.

When news of the assassination hit the headlines, Sweden was traumatized. This was the first killing of its kind ever to take place in modern times in a country that

Every section of society grieved as Sweden fell silent for the funeral of its murdered prime minister Olof Palme

prided itself on its peaceful way of life. Palme himself, who was fifty-nine when he died, had always believed strongly in open government, disliked tight security, and had only used bodyguards to protect him on official occasions. Every year, he and his family had gone on holiday to the island of Gotland, where they had a summer house, and had been left to enjoy themselves undisturbed. In the same way, even in the city, he had been adamant that he should be able to walk about the streets without guards.

Right-wing extremists

After his death, Palme was remembered as a great statesman who had campaigned tirelessly on behalf of the poor, both in Europe and in the Third World. During the Vietnam War, he had called for an end to the fighting, and had become a leading spokesman for peace. During the 1980s, when right-wing governments in America and Britain were in the ascendancy, he had remained a staunch advocate for social democracy. However, during his years in power, his radical policies had made him many enemies, both at home and abroad. There were those who believed that he was in league with the Soviet Union and had not done enough to protect Sweden from Soviet military interventions; in particular, he had not protested strongly enough about Soviet submarines who had ventured into Swedish waters. In fact, before he met his death, he had made arrangements to visit Moscow so as to talk about this issue.

The first man to be arrested for Palme's assassination was Victor Gunnarsson, a right-wing extremist. However, there was very little evidence to show that he had anything to do with the murder, and after a quarrel between the police and the prosecution lawyers, he was released. The next suspect was John Stannerman, a right-wing agitator who was later convicted of a racist murder, and a series of attempted racist murders. However, it then emerged that Stannerman (later known as John Ausonius, or 'The Laser Man' because of the laser gun that he used) had a cast-iron alibi: he had spent the night in question in a prison cell.

Police then followed up a lead given to them by the security services, linking the assassination to a group of Kurdish activists living in Sweden. The investigation was led by Hans Holmer, the head of the Stockholm police force, but it proved fruitless. Meanwhile, the police and security forces were coming under intense criticism for prolonging the investigation and getting nowhere; Holmer was, in later years, removed from office as a result of this criticism.

A social outcast

It was a year and a half before the police came up with a more likely suspect, and even this was to prove problematic. Christer Pettersson, a petty criminal, alcoholic and a drug addict, was picked up in December 1988. Aged forty-two, he was a drifter and social outcast. He had a history of mental illness and violent crime. In 1970, he had killed a youth with a bayonet and had served time in prison for the crime. When he was arrested, Palme's wife, Lisbet, identified him as the killer of her husband. However, she admitted that she had not seen him fire or

A pool of blood marks the spot where Olof Palme was gunned down walking home with his wife from the cinema

hold a gun. In addition, it was not clear why Pettersson had attacked the prime minister. When questioned, he appeared to have no political or other motive for the assassination, and his action did not appear to have been pre-meditated.

In July 1989, Pettersson was convicted of the assassination of Olof Palme and sentenced to life imprisonment. However, the verdict began to be questioned when it emerged that the two judges in the case had recommended that he should be acquitted; on the other hand, six lay assessors had voted for him to be convicted. After much controversy, only three months after the trial, Pettersson's conviction was overturned and he was set free.

Today, it remains unclear whether Pettersson was involved in the assassination or not. Before he died in September 2004, he was reported to have confessed to the murder. However, he never explained why, if he had done it, he had taken this course of action.

Conspiracy theories

The assassination of Olof Palme, which remains unsolved, has continued to generate many conspiracy theories since his death. Pettersson's reported confession has prompted calls for the case to be re-opened, but the Swedish state prosecutor has ruled that, unless something more can be found out about the gun used, the case cannot be brought to court again. Meanwhile, the assassination has been variously explained as the work of anti-apartheid sympathizers, arms traders and freemasons, all of whom – according to the

conspiracy theorists – had a number of reasons to want Palme out of the way.

The anti-apartheid theorists point to the fact that a week before his murder, Palme had made an important speech to the Swedish People's Parliament on the evils of apartheid.

The address had been attended by several leading figures of the anti-apartheid movement, including Oliver Tambo. In the speech, Palme had announced, 'Apartheid cannot be reformed, it has to be eliminated'. A decade later, in 1996, a former South African policeman named Eugene De Kock alleged that the assassin was a former colleague of his in the South African police force, a man named Craig Williamson. According to him, Williamson was also a spy. Williamson's boss, Johannes Coetzee, then announced that the actual murderer was Anthony White, a former Selous Scout from Zimbabwe, formerly Rhodesia. Next, a colleague of White's, Peter Caselton, identified Swedish mercenary soldier, Bertil Wedin, as the real assassin.

Clearly, these allegations had to be investigated, and so the Swedish police travelled to South Africa to try to unravel the story. However, they could not come up with any evidence to sustain the allegations, and returned empty-handed.

The claims that Palme had been murdered by a secret group of arms traders, businessmen and freemasons, who wanted him out of the way because of his well-known opposition to the arms trade, proved equally difficult to substantiate.

To date, the real reason for the

assassination of Olof Palme, one of the most distinguished yet controversial politicians in Swedish history, remains a mystery.

YITZHAK RABIN

The assassination of Yitzhak Rabin, prime minister of Israel, took place on 4 November 1995. Regarded as a 'hawk turned dove', that is, a former military man who later sought peace and compromise, Rabin had made many enemies as well as friends during his long, illustrious career in Israeli politics. After his death, a number of conspiracy theories arose as to what had really taken place, but what remained clear was that hopes for a new era of peace and co-operation between the Israelis and their Arab neighbours in Palestine were set back many years by the assassination.

Yitzhak Rabin was born in Jerusalem, but grew up in Tel Aviv, and became active in Israel's underground army of Jewish settlers in Palestine, known as the Palmach. He went on to have an illustrious military career during the 1948 Israeli War of Independence. He later became chief of staff of the Israeli Defence Forces, which included the army, navy, and air force, and became a hero as a result of Israel's victory in the 1967 war against Egypt, Syria and Jordan. In 1974, he became prime minister of Israel, and gained further honour as the brains behind the famous Entebbe raid, when the army rescued passengers on a plane hijacked by Palestinian terrorists. Later, Rabin resigned from his post as prime minister when his wife was found to have an illegal bank account containing US dollars, which at the time was not allowed in Israel. However, he continued to hold office under the succeeding governments, and in 1992 once again became prime minister.

In his last term of office, Rabin played a more conciliatory part in the Arab–Israeli conflict than he had previously. Under the Oslo Accords, his government began to recognize Palestinian rights over parts of the West Bank and Gaza Strip, and worked towards peace between the two nations, for which he later received the Nobel Prize. However, Rabin's new initiative earned him many critics among the right-wing Israeli establishment, who saw him as conceding ground to the Arabs and giving away territory that rightfully belonged to Israel.

One such critic was Yigal Amir. Amir was born in 1970 to an orthodox Jewish family who had emigrated to Israel from the Yemen. As a young man, he trained in the Jewish army, and went on to study law at university, where he became involved in right-wing politics. He organized demonstrations against the Oslo Accords, which he saw as a terrible betrayal of Israeli interests. However, once it became clear that the peace process was well under way and unlikely to be turned back, he decided to take matters into his own hands.

Amir acquired a Beretta semi-automatic pistol, and waited for the prime minister in a quiet parking lot as he attended a pro-peace rally in a Tel Aviv square. Once Rabin came within range, he shot the prime minister, also wounding a security guard who was standing close by. Rabin was rushed to hospital but it was too late to save him. One

Yitzhak Rabin in heated discussion, the year of his death

of the bullets had penetrated his lung, and he had lost an enormous amount of blood.

Amir was immediately apprehended, and taken into custody. He later received a sentence of life imprisonment.

Despite Rabin's unpopularity among the right-wing establishment, the assassination was roundly condemned by most Israelis.

Today, the Kings of Israel Square, where Rabin died, has been re-named after him, and his death is popularly commemorated each year by a national memorial day.

After the assassination, conspiracy theories as to what lay behind the crime began to surface. There were rumours of anomalies in the police and medical reports

Right-winger Yigal Amir got hold of a Beretta semi-automatic and waited in a parking lot until Yitzhak Rabin came by

on the incident, which had been hushed up and covered over. For example, it was suggested that the surgeon found a gunshot wound to Rabin's chest, whereas Amir had apparently shot him in the back. And although Rabin apparently died of blood loss, as well as the lung wound, his wife reported that he did not appear to be bleeding at all directly after he had been shot. This led some to believe that Rabin had actually been shot by someone else other than the gunman, possibly after he arrived at the hospital.

There was also some evidence to show that Amir was not a lone killer, but had been

Among the world leaders who attended Rabin's funeral were presidents Hosni Mubarak of Egypt and Bill Clinton of the USA

acting as part of a group. Conspiracy theorists pointed to the assassin's close friendship with Avishai Raviv, an agent of the Israeli Secret Service (known as Shin Bet or Shabak), and to his political activities with his brother, Hagai, and a friend, Dror Adani.

Several commentators also suggested that the shooting was a set-up, staged to look like an attempt on Rabin's life and thus increase his popularity with the public, but that it had gone disastrously wrong as other factions took advantage of the situation to actually assassinate him.

After the assassination, Amir was imprisoned and began a relationship by mail and telephone with a supporter, a Russian Jewish immigrant to Israel named Larisa Trembovler. After many conflicts with the authorities, Trembovler, a mother of four, divorced her husband and married Amir. Amir then agitated to be allowed private conjugal visits with his wife, so that he could father a child by her. However, this was disallowed by the prison authorities as a security risk. Recently, Amir has been on hunger strike and has also applied to enter an artificial insemination programme.

Meanwhile, ten years after the event, theories about the assassination of Yitzhak Rabin continue to abound, and look set to proliferate for the foreseeable future. It could be that the differing accounts of what happened on that fateful day were simply the result of confusion and dismay; or, as some believe, the true story may be altogether more sinister.

PARK CHUNG HEE

Park Chung Hee, the president of South Korea from 1961 to 1970, is the man credited with transforming the country from a backward rural economy into a modern industrial state. On 26 October 1979, he was assassinated by the chief of the Korea Central Intelligence Agency, Kim Jaegyu. To date, it remains a matter of some conjecture as to whether Kim Jaegyu shot the president because he was envious of his political power, or whether – as his supporters claim – he wanted to rid the country of a man he considered to be an oppressive dictator.

Military coup

Park Chung Hee was born in Seonsan, a small town in the province of North Gyeongsang, Korea, on 30 September 1917. He attended school in Daegu, one of the major cities in Korea, and went on to study at a military academy. After teaching for some years, he became a soldier, fighting the communist forces of China under Chairman Mao.

After the Second World War, in which Japan was defeated, Park aligned himself with the left, and rebelled against the Korean government, with the support of the American authorities. He narrowly escaped being put to death. Later, he became a colonel in the army, and led a military coup against the established government in 1961. Two years later, the military government was replaced by a civilian one, and Park won the election, as leader of the Democratic Republican Party.

From that point, Park led a campaign to transform South Korea from an under-developed, peasant economy in the shadow of its more powerful neighbour, North Korea, to a modern industrialized state. He was much criticized in some quarters for his dictatorial style, and for fragmenting the traditional cultural patterns of the nation, but even his opponents had to admit that, under his government, incomes of ordinary people increased to a massive degree. Those who had been living in grinding poverty in rural areas now found themselves moving into towns and cities, with access to new jobs, housing, education and medical facilities. The rise in the standard of living was extremely rapid, and South Korea is still regarded, to this day, as something of a miracle – in terms of its economy, if not its democratic development.

A brutal dictatorship

Despite overseeing his country's increasing prosperity, Park made himself very unpopular in many ways, in particular by resuming friendly relations with Japan. The Japanese had at one time colonized Korea, and the Japanese regime there was remembered as brutal and oppressive.

Park argued that without economic aid from Japan, as well as from America, the country could not rebuild itself; however, his strategy was not appreciated by the electorate, who still had bitter memories of the Japanese, and in subsequent elections, he did not do well. Recognizing his weakness, in 1972 he took the controversial step of altering the country's constitution in such a way that he

Copied by his security guard, Park Chung Hee dons traditional paddyfield garb for Farmers Day in South Korea

South Korea celebrated Armed Forces Day in 1963 as 20,000 troops marched in perfect order past hardliner Park Chung Hee

virtually became a dictator. He banned all forms of opposition to his regime, which grew more and more oppressive as the years went by. Dissidents were regularly imprisoned and tortured. Elections continued to be held, but they were not free and fair, and South Korea became known throughout the western world for its human rights abuses.

A missed target

Not surprisingly, there were many opponents to what had now become an oppressive dictatorship, and on 15 August 1974, a North Korean agent living in Japan, Mun Segwang, attempted to assassinate the president. Park was giving a speech to more than a thousand people at the National Theatre in Seoul, to mark the country's Liberation Day. In a dramatic attack, a gunman ran down the centre aisle of the theatre, firing a pistol at the stage. Park was not injured, because the podium on which he was standing was bulletproof. However, a stray bullet hit his wife Yuk Yeongsu in the head. A 17-year-old girl who was present was also shot and died. The women were rushed immediately to hospital, while the resolute Park continued to deliver his speech. Afterwards, however, he followed his wife to the hospital. Yuk Yeongsu died there, six hours later.

The assassin tried to flee, but security guards opened fire on him, and he was wounded. He was then captured and later identified as Mun Segwang, a 22-year-old Korean living in Osaka, Japan. A member of the Korean Youth League, who opposed the Park regime, he had travelled to South Korea on a false Japanese passport, and later told the authorities that he had been instructed to kill the president by North Korean agents he had met in Japan.

The agents had said that they had been instructed by Kim Il Sung to arrange for the assassination of the president. Whether this story was true or not remains a matter of some controversy to this day.

Four months after the killing of Yuk Yeongsu, Mun Segwang was convicted of the crime and executed. The attempt severely strained relations between North Korea and South Korea, since the South Koreans believed that Mun Segwang had indeed been instructed by the North Korean authorities.

Shoot-out in the bunker

Five years later, on 26 October 1979, there was another attempt on the president's life. This time it was successful. The assassin was Kim Jaegyu, the head of security forces in the state, and formerly a close friend of the president. He had opposed Park Chung Hee's dictatorial style of leadership, and had stood against him before in elections, narrowly escaping being imprisoned when Park changed the constitution to suit his own ends. The assassination took place during a meeting at a secret security residence in Seoul.

On that day, the men had met to discuss opposition to the regime, in particular student riots that had taken place in Pusan. According to some sources, Kim Jaegyu was in a defensive frame of mind, and was afraid of losing his job because of the disturbances. A bitter argument broke out between Kim and the president's bodyguard, Cha Chi Chol, whom some said had replaced Kim as the president's right-hand man. Kim walked out and went to fetch a gun, and on returning to the room, opened fire on Cha Chi Col. Cha ran away, hiding behind some furniture, at which point Kim shot the president in the chest. Kim then dragged Cha out, and shot him in the stomach.

After that, he shot the president in the head, and continued to fire until both men were dead. A fight ensued between the president's bodyguards and Kim's men, in which a total of five more men perished.

Because of the chaotic nature of the killing, it was generally assumed that Kim had acted in a fit of violent rage, and that there was no real political motivation for his actions – the theory was that he had shot the president and his bodyguard because he was furious about being sidelined. However, there were those that questioned this version of events, and over time the circumstances of the assassination began to be reassessed. The fact that the government were unwilling to release details of what had gone on, and that there were few who dared to voice their opinions about the matter, meant that this re-evaluation was very slow in coming.

Brutal murderer or liberator?

Directly after the assassination, the country was thrown into chaos, and eventually the military seized power, under the leadership of army general Chun Doo-hwan. Chun's government saw to it that Kim Jaegyu was brought to justice for the murder. On 24 May 1980, Kim Jaegyu was put to death.

For many years, there was little comment, analysis or information about the assassination, but now, over two decades after the event, it is beginning to be reviewed.

Kim Young-hee, Kim Jaegyu's widow, presented a special commission for democratization with a petition, asking them to collect new information about what really happened. According to some sources, Kim Jaegyu kept a diary in prison while awaiting his trial, claiming that he wanted to end the tyranny of the regime and restore democracy to the country. The diary also shows that he was a devout Buddhist who expressed an indifference to wealth, position and power. Newly released information also suggests that there were several high-ranking figures in the country who had petitioned for his release, including several Catholic priests and political leaders. Not only this, there was a campaign to try to stop the execution, supported by at least a thousand people, some of them prominent members of the opposition. After Kim's execution, his supporters erected a national monument to him in Kwangju, Kyunggi Province.

At the same time, Park Geun-hye, Park Chung Hee's daughter, has led a campaign to discredit Kim Jaegyu, saying that he had killed the president for his own political ends, not so as to end the tyranny of the regime and restore democracy in South Korea. They point out that, at the time, Kim was the head of the Central Intelligence Agency, which was known for its brutality in suppressing those who wanted to restore democracy in South Korea. They also argue that the assassination of the president was anything but democratic, and set back South Korea's political agenda for many years, at a time during the late 1970s when the movement for democracy was beginning to gain ground. In fact, in the year Park Chun

Hee was assassinated, there had been a record number of protests and demonstrations against his regime, which was, of course, why the fatal meeting had been convened in the first place.

Today, Park Chung Hee is widely respected in South Korea as a great statesman, whose economic programme brought prosperity to millions in a nation that was extremely poor. However, the circumstances of his assassination are still the subject of much controversy, and whatever the outcome of future investigations, remind us that South Korea's current wealth was achieved at some cost – not least that of freedom, democracy and free speech.

HENDRIK VERWOERD

Hendrik Verwoerd is remembered as the architect of apartheid. During his rule as prime minister of South Africa, from 1958 to 1966, he did everything in his power to ensure the ascendancy of the white population in the country, including moving thousands of black people into 'homeland' areas, or Bantustans, in order to achieve a whites-only central state. There were two assassination attempts on his life, the second of which was successful. On 6 September 1966, he was stabbed to death by Dimitri Tsafendas, who was later declared to be suffering from mental illness. Today, Verwoerd's legacy is generally held to be a destructive one, which caused immense suffering to millions of black people at the time of his leadership, and whose effects still reverberate in the country today; however, there are still those in South Africa who believe him to have been one of the country's great statesmen.

Hendrik Frensch Verwoerd was born in Weesp, near Amsterdam in the Netherlands, on 8 September 1901. He was the second son of shopkeepers Wilhelmus Johannes Verwoerd and his wife Anje Strik.

Wilhelmus was very religious, and sympathetic to the situation of the Afrikaners in South Africa after the war with the British there. In 1903, the family moved to South Africa, where they settled for ten years before moving to Bulawayo, Rhodesia (as it then was) so that Wilhelmus could pursue his calling as an evangelist in the Dutch Reformed Church. The family remained in Bulawayo for four years before returning to South Africa, where they lived in Brandtfort, in the Orange Free State.

Nazi ideology

Hendrik was a very able pupil at the schools he attended, and as a young man shone at university, where he studied theology, psychology and philosophy at the University of Stellenbosch. He gained a doctorate, and was offered a scholarship at Oxford University in England, but turned it down because he and his family had a deep hostility to the British. Instead, he went to Germany to study, where he met his wife. He was also influenced by the prevailing political climate there, and studied under Dr Eugene Fischer, an anthropologist who advocated racial segregation and genocide. Fischer's ideology also influenced another fast-rising national leader, Adolf Hitler,

Henrik Verwoerd leaves South Africa House, London in 1963 after a press conference promoting the goals of apartheid

who expanded on the theme in his book, *Mein Kampf*.

In 1927, Verwoerd returned to South Africa and took up a post at Stellenbosch University, eventually becoming Professor of Sociology there. During this time he became involved in politics, campaigning for racial segregation, and for South Africa to become a republic. In 1937 he became editor of the newspaper *Die Transvaler*, which gave him further opportunity to disseminate his ideas. The newspaper carried articles denouncing Jews who held prominent positions in the county, criticizing mixed marriages between whites and blacks, and generally advancing the extreme right-wing ideas that he had picked up in Germany.

The outbreak of the Second World War caused a great deal of antipathy to the Germans worldwide, and Verwoerd's newspaper was accused by a rival paper, the *Johannesburg Star*, of being pro-Nazi. Verwoerd took the proprietor of the *Star* to court, but lost the case. Once the war was over, Verwoerd's hostility to the British became even more intense, and his newspaper famously ignored the visit to South Africa of the British royal family, mentioning only that some 'congestion' had been caused in the streets by 'visitors from overseas'.

Architect of apartheid

Verwoerd was a staunch supporter of the right-wing National Party in South Africa, and when they came into power, he left his position as editor of *Die Transvaler* and began to work in politics full time. By 1950, he had become a member of the Cabinet, and helped to mastermind the establishment of the black 'homelands', or *Bantustans*, in which over eighty thousand black Africans were displaced. They were forced to move from mixed urban centres such as Sophiatown and Newclare to black-only townships in Soweto. At the same time, Verwoerd set up a separate education system for blacks, limiting the curriculum to basic skills in reading, writing and arithmetic. According to him, black people would not need more than this, since their destiny was to be 'hewers of wood and drawers of water'. In this way, by segregating blacks from the white population in townships, and denying them the same educational and economic opportunities as whites, Verwoerd sought to ensure – and succeeded in ensuring – that the Afrikaners would always have the upper hand in South Africa.

In 1958, Verwoerd became prime minister of South Africa. After holding a referendum in which only white people were allowed to vote, South Africa became a republic. The National Party was also able to gain a majority in the national elections. Given this 'mandate', Verwoerd then took South Africa out of the Commonwealth, further separating his country from the democratic values of Europe.

It then began to become clear that South Africa was being shunned by many countries around the world, as a result of its blatantly racist social system. Accordingly, Verwoerd tried to present apartheid in a new light: he argued that black South Africans belonged to separate 'tribal nations' with their own homelands, where they could have 'equal' political rights and develop their own culture in parallel with that of white culture. This was a more subtle argument than the previous Afrikaner theory that black people were inherently inferior to whites, and should therefore serve their masters, and attracted more white followers to the cause of apartheid.

However, events in South Africa belied this apparently more humanitarian approach. As black people began to protest about the reality of life in the townships – in which they were forced to subsist in poverty, under harsh working conditions, subjected to police brutality and unable to travel around freely – it became clear that Verwoerd's 'separate-but-equal' policy was a myth.

Brutal regime

Under Verwoerd's leadership, the government of South Africa became known as one of the most brutal regimes of the twentieth century. In the Sharpeville Massacre of 21 March 1960, police opened fire on a crowd of protesters, killing many and injuring hundreds more.

The protesters had gathered to complain about the law forcing them to carry 'dompas', or pass books. Verwoerd also outlawed political opposition to his policies, banning the African National Congress and imprisoning black leaders such as Nelson Mandela.

Not surprisingly, Verwoerd became an extremely unpopular figure during his prime ministership, and there were many who wanted him out of the way. However, curiously enough, it was not political opposition but mental instability that appears to have motivated both attempts on

his life, the second of which was to prove all too successful.

Shot in the face

The first attempt came on 9 April 1960, when Verwoerd was shot while attending the Union Exposition on the Witwatersrand, to mark the Jubilee of the Union of South Africa. He made a speech and then went back to his seat. Not long afterwards, a middle-aged man approached him, called out Verwoerd's name and fired a gun at him, at point-blank range. Two bullets hit Verwoerd in the face, one in his right cheek, and one in his right ear. Colonel G.M. Harrison, the president of the Witwatersrand Agricultural Society, leapt up and knocked the gun from the man's hand. The man was overpowered by other members of the audience, and taken to the police station. Verwoerd was rushed to hospital, where surgeons removed both bullets, fearing that he might lose his hearing and his sense of balance. However, the operations were successful, and Verwoerd soon returned to work. The surgeons agreed that he had been very lucky, and had a slightly larger calibre gun been used, he would have lost his life or been permanently disabled.

The would-be assassin was David Pratt, a 52-year-old farmer and father of three who was a member of the Agricultural Society. He had been present in Verwoerd's company a number of times, and had in fact sat next to Verwoerd at the opening of the exhibition. Although at first it appeared that Pratt had a political motivation to kill Verwoerd, whom he described as 'the epitome of apartheid', it transpired during his trial that he suffered from epilepsy, and was mentally confused as a result. He was declared to be insane and committed to a mental hospital in Blomfontein. Pratt hanged himself in October 1961, a few months after his incarceration.

Six years later, Verwoerd was not so lucky. This time, he was due to make an important speech in parliament, following talks with the prime minister of Lesotho. This was the first time that the leader of a black state had met for talks with the South African prime minister. On 6 September 1966, Verwoerd came into the House of Assembly and took his seat, nodding hello to various acquaintances as he did. At that moment Dimitri Tsafendas, dressed in the uniform of a parliamentary messenger, appeared, and walked quickly over to the prime minister. He drew a large sheath knife from under his clothes, and took off the sheath. Raising his hand high into the air, he plunged the knife into Verwoerd's chest, stabbing him a total of four times.

Overpowered

When his colleagues realized what was happening, they rushed to help Verwoerd, and pulled Tsafendas away, rapidly overpowering him. There were four doctors of medicine present, all of them members of parliament. They did what they could to save him, one of them administering the kiss of life. Verwoerd's wife, who was watching from the gallery, ran down to be with her husband as they waited for an ambulance to arrive. Verwoerd was rushed to Groote Schuur Hospital, where he was pronounced dead on arrival. He died from a punctured lung and heart and his death sent a tidal wave of rumours sweeping across South Africa, setting every community abuzz. What was the nature of the man who had assassinated Verwoerd?

Paranoid schizophrenic

Later that year, Tsafendas came to trial. He was a 48-year-old man, the son of a Greek Cypriot father and a black Mozambique mother. He suffered from mental illness, and had been diagnosed as a paranoid schizophrenic. He was convinced that there was a giant tapeworm in his body that was eating him up from the inside, and that it often spoke to him, telling him what to do. On this occasion, so he alleged, the tapeworm had told him to kill Verwoerd.

Another odd feature of Tsafendas' history was that, although he was dark-skinned, he had been classified, under South Africa's race laws, as white. He had apparently fallen in love with a coloured woman, and had applied to be re-classified as coloured. Whether this had any bearing or not on his assassination of the prime minister was unclear, but after only three days, the judge, Justice Beyers, decided that Tsafendas' mind was disordered to such a degree that he was unfit to stand trial. Beyers ordered Tsafendas to be kept away from society, 'in a place of safety', and accordingly, he was taken to prison, and then to a psychiatric hospital, where he remained until his death in 1999.

Speculation still arises over Tsafendas and his motives for the murder. Henk van Woerden produced a biography, *A Mouthful of Glass*, and in 2003 Anthony Sher wrote a play which was performed at the Almeida theatre in London.

CHAPTER TWO

SHOOTING THE MESSENGER

Anyone who dares to challenge the status quo, be it for a great cause or simply for personal advancement, risks hostility and violence from those around them. This is never more true than in the case of the radicals and revolutionaries who have shaped the course of their nations' histories around the world.

Perhaps the most illustrious of these leaders was Martin Luther King, the church minister and civil rights leader who came to embody the hopes of many Americans that black and white people could live together in equality, justice and freedom in the United States of America. Despite – or perhaps because of – his extraordinary talent for inspiring American citizens to work together for a better world, by the time he died he was living in fear of assassination. He was afraid that he would be murdered either by government security forces, who at the time he died were tracking his every move, or by racists bitterly opposed to his dream of a new, racially integrated America. In the end, his fears proved justified, and he was shot in 1968 as he stood on the balcony of his motel the night after giving one of his most rousing speeches, at the height of his fame and influence.

In the same way, another of America's great black leaders, Malcolm X, met his death as the result of an assassination, just as he had

feared. In his case, the assassination threats came not only from government and political groups opposed to his views, but from factions within the black power Nation of Islam movement itself. To this day, it is unclear whether his murder was planned by the CIA or by elements within the Nation of Islam – or possibly, by a combination of both.

Assassinations of radical figures such as Pancho Villa, the Mexican revolutionary and bandit, are hardly surprising. These are men who have lived and died by the sword, whose lives have been characterized by armed conflict, bloody battles and fierce raids; men whose lives have been as brutal as they have been brave. What was surprising in the case of Villa was that he had not been killed before; by the time he was assassinated, he had stopped campaigning, and was living quietly on his ranch at Durango, having ended his wild ways and built a hospital, school and chapel in the town.

In the same way, the death of Rasputin, the womanizing, drunken monk who befriended the Russian royal family and scandalized the Russian court, came as no great shock. Rasputin's licentious behaviour, and the influence he appeared to have over the czarina, brought the whole Russian aristocracy into disrepute, and it was only a matter of time before they plotted his death.

However, it did not prove easy to kill this 'bear of a man'; and his uncanny ability to withstand poisoning, bullets and drowning, gave credence to the idea that the 'evil monk' did, indeed, have some magical powers not given to ordinary mortals.

Here are the stories of these men, from the great and the good, to the wild and the wicked, who have led turbulent lives and met violent deaths at the hands of assassins.

MARTIN LUTHER KING

The assassination of Martin Luther King on 4 April 1968 marked a turning point in the history of America. On that day, the country's leading civil rights activist was shot dead on the balcony of a motel in Memphis, Tennessee. At the time he died, King's campaign to bring equal rights for black people had achieved an extraordinary change of heart among the mass of Americans, and the day before, he had made a rousing speech to an ecstatic crowd of thousands. During the speech, King had referred to the constant threats that were being made on his life, and had hinted that he himself might not live to see the time when America became a 'Promised Land' of people united in peace, freedom and justice.

Sadly, he was proved right when, the following evening, he was shot dead. The person convicted of his murder was James Earl Ray, an ex-convict and open racist. However, there were some – including members of King's family – who did not believe that Ray was responsible, and

suspected that the FBI and CIA were behind the killing. Whatever the truth, King's death spelled the end of an optimistic period in American society, in which people began to hope that the racial discrimination and economic inequality, which had for so long divided the country, would one day come to an end.

Civil disobedience

Michael King was born in Atlanta, Georgia, the son of a Baptist minister and a teacher. His parents later changed his name to Martin. As a young man, King followed his father into a career in the church. After studying for several years, he received a doctorate and then went to work as a minister in Montgomery, Alabama. King married Coretta Scott in 1953, and the couple went on to have four children, all of whom eventually became civil rights workers.

King quickly attracted a large congregation and became an important spokesperson for black people in the area. He was vociferous in his condemnation of the racist laws of the South, which required black people to live separately from, and take second place to, the white population. A staunch supporter of desegregation, he made his views widely known, even though he knew that there would be retaliation from white separatists. In 1955, after the famous incident in which Rosa Parks, a black woman, refused to give up her seat to a white man on the bus, he helped to organize a boycott of the buses in Montgomery. Soon the bus company was ordered to change its rules.

In the years that followed, King became a

The 1960s were a momentous decade for US civil rights: here leading lights Martin Luther King and Malcolm X shake hands

Witnessed by a crowd of 50,000–100,000, King's coffin went through Atlanta on a wooden farm wagon drawn by two mules

leading proponent of the growing US civil rights movement. Taking Mahatma Gandhi as his example, he began to lead protests in the southern city of Birmingham, Alabama, putting forward a policy of civil disobedience and stressing that all direct action should be non-violent. Nonetheless, he was imprisoned for his activities. Also, a number of bomb attacks were made on the activists' headquarters, in an attempt to intimidate the civil rights campaigners. However, King and his followers were not deterred, and went on to assist in organizing the huge civil rights march on Washington in 1963. This was the event that King chose to deliver his famous speech about his dream of a united America, where black people could live side by side with white people in peace and equality.

In 1964, King received the Nobel Peace Prize, and went on to campaign successfully for black people's voting rights. He then began to agitate against the US war in Vietnam, which made him new enemies in the government and the media. He also brought people's attention to the extreme poverty in which many Americans, both black and white, were forced to live, which was another issue that the authorities would have preferred him to ignore.

Death threats

During this period, King was under constant surveillance from the FBI. Yet despite the fact that there were daily threats on his life, the US intelligence forces did not offer him a great deal of protection. It was this lack of enthusiasm for ensuring the security of one of America's leading political figures that caused rumours to spread when King was later assassinated.

At 6 p.m. on the evening of 4 April 1968, King was standing on the balcony of the Lorraine Motel in Memphis, Tennessee. Without warning, a lone gunman hidden in the bushes below shot him at close range. King was wounded in the jaw, collapsed and was rushed to hospital, where he died a few hours later.

The police seemed unable to find out anything about King's assassin, and came under a great deal of pressure to do so. However, it was not until two months later that an escaped prisoner named James Earl Ray was picked up in Britain. He had been travelling under a false passport. Police arrested him, interrogated him and sent him to Tennessee to face charges. There, on 10 March 1969, Ray confessed to the murder of Martin Luther King. He was charged, tried, convicted and finally sentenced to a prison term of ninety-nine years.

Killer framed?

Later, Ray took back his confession, alleging that he had only pleaded guilty to escape the death penalty, on the advice of his attorney. He also said that his attorney had pressurized him because he wanted to make money from a movie deal. Ray accused his brother, Johnny, and a Canadian smuggler named 'Raoul' for the murder, but his account was full of inconsistencies. In 1994, investigators found a retired auto worker in upstate New York who matched a photo of 'Raoul' given to them by Ray. The man was cleared of involvement, but sadly, the accusation ruined his life, and he never managed to shake off the stigma. The questions about King's death remained unanswered until, in 1997, a House Select Committee finally concluded that there may have been a conspiracy, but that Ray had definitely shot King. Ray continued to maintain that he had not, until his death in prison on 23 April 1998.

Because of the establishment's ambivalent attitude towards Martin Luther King, rumours about his assassination still persisted. King's son, Dexter King, was convinced that his father had been killed by FBI agents and made strenuous efforts to prove his theory. He pointed out that there were various items of evidence at the scene of the crime, and findings from the investigation, that cast doubt on Ray's guilt. For example, ballistic tests conducted after the assassination could not prove that the rifle was the murder weapon. In addition, Ray's personal history showed that although he was a burglar he had no previous record of violence. It was also doubtful that he was a good enough marksman to hit his target. In fact, Ray's record showed that, as a criminal, he was not very able, and would not have had the intelligence or the courage to pull off the assassination.

Other theories were that Ray had acted as a hit man for the FBI, under the direction of assistant director Cartha DeLoach, who had masterminded the plot. According to this theory, Ray had travelled to Memphis to take part in a bank robbery while King was in town. Ray had just happened to be staying in a rooming house next door to King's hotel on the evening when King was shot by an FBI gunman hiding in a shrubbery nearby. Afterward, the FBI had planted the murder weapon, a Remington rifle, in Ray's car and framed him for the murder.

Unknown conspirators

In the years after King's assassination, his family went on to advance their theory that the FBI was responsible for murdering him. Martin Luther's son, Dexter King, publicly met with Ray in 1997, shook the prisoner's hand, and pledged support for his campaign for a trial. Two years later, Coretta Scott King launched a civil trial against Memphis bar owner Lloyd Jowers and 'other unknown conspirators' who were thought to have committed the assassination. Jowers was found guilty on that occasion, but the King family were only awarded a symbolic sum of $100, and a later investigation found no evidence of Jowers' involvement in any plot.

To date, it appears that no hard evidence has been found to link the US security services to the assassination of Martin Luther King. However, there remain important questions about the FBI's attitude towards King when he was alive. In particular its attempts to smear him as a communist, and its constant, intrusive surveillance of his daily activities, has undoubtedly caused some to question their claim that King was shot by a petty criminal.

Whoever did the deed, and whatever the truth of the matter, there is no doubt that the assassination of Martin Luther King traumatized the American nation, in much the same way that the killing of John F. Kennedy did. King's courageous campaign,

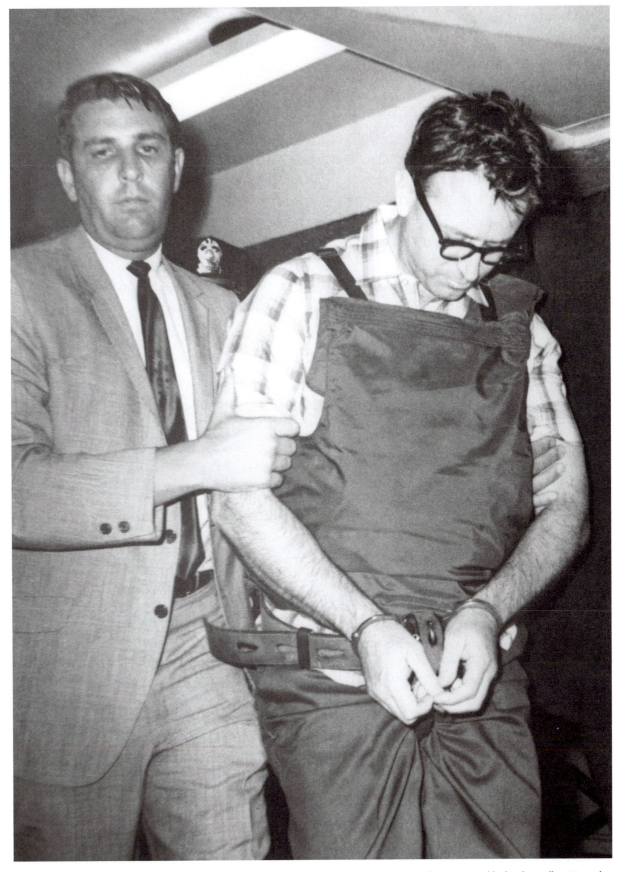

Head bowed and hands manacled, James Earl Ray was charged with killing Martin Luther King and led to his cell in Memphis

in the face of so much opposition, had brought genuine hope for peace, justice and equality to a divided nation; and for many, when he was assassinated, his vision of a united America also died.

MALCOLM X

The assassination of Malcolm X, the charismatic Black Muslim leader, on 21 February 1965, remains the subject of much controversy. At the time of his murder, Malcolm X was one of the two leading black political figures in America. The other, of course, was Martin Luther King, who was assassinated just a couple of years later. Many believed that, like King, Malcolm X had been killed by the CIA because he was a threat to the security of the nation, preaching a strong anti-white message and criticizing American society as fundamentally racist. Whether or not this was the case, or whether he was killed by a rival faction within his own political group, the Nation of Islam, is still not entirely clear. However, the fact remains that the two most important black leaders of their generation, Martin Luther King and Malcolm X, both came to a violent end for daring to speak out against the injustices that had been endured by black people in America since the days of slavery.

Ruthless hustler

Malcolm X was born Malcolm Little in Omaha, Nebraska. His father was a Baptist minister and a leading figure in a repatriation movement known as the 'Marcus Garvey Back To Africa' movement.

As a young man, Malcolm X turned to petty crime as a drug dealer and pimp, moving around the country and working in the black ghettoes of New York and other major American cities. He gained a reputation as a hard man, a ruthless hustler and snappy dresser, who would stop at nothing to get what he wanted in life.

At the age of eighteen, he was convicted as a burglar, and went to prison. In jail, he was introduced to the books of Elijah Muhammad, a Black Muslim leader. He became a Muslim and changed his name to Malcolm X. On his release in 1952, he settled in Detroit and became a Muslim minister at the temple of the Nation of Islam, moving to New York two years later.

Nation of Islam

The Nation of Islam was a radical black political group led by Elijah Muhammad. Muhammad's son-in-law Raymond Sharrief was set to become his heir. However, Malcolm X soon became a rival to Sharrief, due to his intelligence, high level of commitment and generally magnetic character. Soon, relations between the two became tense, and eventually Malcolm X left the Nation of Islam to found his own movement, the Organisation of Afro-American Unity, during the summer of 1964.

During this time, Malcolm X had become a reviled figure in the mainstream American media and was routinely vilified for his anti-white statements. However, as he began to travel around the world, especially to Africa, he began to adopt a more integrationist perspective. After meeting anti-apartheid

Malcom X addressing a rally on 14 May 1963, in Harlem, in support of desegregation in Birmingham, Alabama

activists in South Africa, he became convinced that black and white people could work together to achieve political change. This realization was another reason that he split with the Nation of Islam to form his own organization.

Shortly after forming the Organisation of Afro-American Unity, Malcolm X returned to Africa and spent several months out of the US, finally coming back in November 1964. While he was in Africa, he complained that he was being followed by CIA agents. In Cairo, he became seriously ill, and there were rumours that he might have had his food poisoned on purpose. On his return, the animosity between himself and Muhammad's followers intensified, to the point where death threats were issued against him. By this time, Malcolm X knew that his life was in danger: either from the CIA, or from his erstwhile colleagues in the Nation of Islam.

Multiple bullet wounds

A week before his eventual assassination Malcolm X's house in Queens, New York was firebombed. At the time Malcolm assumed that the Nation of Islam was behind the attack. The following day, 15 February, he made a speech at the Audubon Ballroom in Harlem. As he spoke, a scuffle broke out in the audience. Six days later Malcolm returned to the Audubon, once more to make a speech. Mysteriously, all the others speakers scheduled to appear had cancelled. Before it was time for Malcolm to speak, and while talking to friends in the backstage area, he is alleged to have confided that he wasn't sure that it had been the Nation of

Islam that had been behind the firebombing of his house. He had suspicions that, in fact, it might have been, since relations between the two organizations had deteriorated rapidly. Having expressed his doubts, he went out to the podium and began to give his speech.

Malcolm X draws various reactions from his audience in a Harlem rally in 1963

At around 3.05pm Eastern Standard Time a disturbance broke out in the crowd of four hundred. A man yelled, 'Get your hand outta my pocket! Don't be messin' with my pockets!' Then a smoke bomb went off at the back of the auditorium, causing widespread panic and confusion. Malcolm X's bodyguards moved forward to calm the crowd, but meanwhile, taking advantage of the chaos, a black man came running towards the stage and shot Malcolm in the chest with a sawn-off shotgun from point-

Should he have risked appearing so publically? Tragically, the second attempt on Malcom X's life within a week was successful

blank range. Two other men quickly charged towards the stage as well, and fired handguns at Malcolm. The three assassins then attempted to escape, but the angry crowd managed to capture one of the two men with handguns. The man was later identified as Talmadge Hayer.

Malcolm X's bodyguard Gene Roberts, who was actually an undercover policeman, attempted to resuscitate Malcolm but to no avail. There was no doubt that Malcolm X was dead. The autopsy was performed by New York City's Chief Medical Examiner, Dr Milton Helpern, and found that 'the cause of death was multiple shotgun pellet and bullet wounds in the chest, heart and aorta'. He had been hit by eight shotgun slugs and nine bullets.

Three assassins

Malcolm's funeral was held in Harlem on 27 February 1965 at the Faith Temple Church of God in Christ (now Child's Memorial Temple Church of God in Christ). Fifteen hundred people attended the ceremony, and afterwards his friends took the shovels away from the waiting gravediggers and buried him themselves, at the Ferncliff Cemetery in Hartsdale, New York. Soon, three people were arrested for his murder: Nation of Islam members Talmadge Hayer, Norman 3X Butler, and Thomas 15X Johnson. All three men were convicted of first-degree murder in March 1966 and received prison sentences.

On the face of it, this was a clear case of infighting between black radicals, resulting in the death of one of their greatest leaders. Gradually, however, rumours began to circulate that all may not have been as it seemed, and that there was more to the story than met the eye.

CIA or Nation of Islam?

The suspicion centred around the notion that, while Malcolm X had indeed been assassinated by members of the Nation of Islam, these men were actually being manipulated by government forces. When the case was investigated more thoroughly, it was found that several members of the highly secretive Bureau of Special Services (BOSS) were present in the audience at the time of the killing. One of these undercover detectives, Gene Roberts, was one of Malcolm X's bodyguards at the time of the killing. This seemed suspicious enough, but then, on 25 February 1965, four days after the assassination of Malcolm X, one of his senior followers, Leon 4X Ameer, announced that he was convinced his life was in danger. He then died of an apparent overdose of sleeping pills. It is alleged that he had been on the point of revealing evidence of government involvement in Malcolm's murder, and that the security forces had been behind his apparent suicide.

Further speculation surrounds the question of who really carried out the killing. Talmadge Hayer was certainly guilty, but there was a great deal of evidence to suggest that his co-defendants were not even present at the Audubon Ballroom at the time of the assassination. Some believe that the two other killers escaped, and have to this day never been brought to justice. Not only this, but Talmadge Hayer has stated that he was never a member of the Nation of Islam and that he was hired to commit the murder. He also claimed that the man who hired him was not a Muslim, which suggests he may have been hired by a government agent.

Today, it is unclear whether it was the American government or the Nation of Islam that was really behind the murder. It is probably true to say that few people at the FBI shed many tears for Malcolm X; however, that does not necessarily mean that they ordered his murder, and there has been little concrete evidence to show this was the case. It has also been pointed out that the Nation of Islam was locked in a struggle with Malcolm X, and that its leaders such as Elijah Muhammad and his eventual successor Louis Farrakhan had publicly called for Malcolm's elimination. Some commentators believe that both parties are implicated: that the killers were Black Muslims, and they were supported by security agents. Whatever the truth, the fact is that Malcolm X, like John F. Kennedy before him and Martin Luther King not long afterwards, was cut down in his prime. For

One of the great heroes of the Mexican revolution, Pancho Villa helped overthrow the country's corrupt dictator, Porfirio Diaz

many, his death marked the end of a period of optimism and hope during the 1960s that black and white people could one day live peacefully together in America.

PANCHO VILLA

Many years after his death, the Mexican revolutionary leader Pancho Villa has become an emblem of the wild spirit of his country. One of the most prominent leaders of the Mexican Revolution, he helped to overthrow the corrupt dictator Porfirio Diaz in 1910, and went on to defend the revolution after its new leader had been executed. In 1920, he gave up fighting and retired, only to be assassinated three years later. Today, opinions differ as to why he was murdered after his revolutionary activities had ceased, and some have suggested that he was in league with foreign powers. However, to this day he remains one of the great heroes of the Mexican Revolution.

The outlaw

Born Jose Doroteo Arango Arambula in 1877, 1878 or 1879 (there is some controversy as to the exact year of his birth), he later adopted the name Francisco Villa as a 'nom de guerre', and became known by the diminutive form of Francisco, Pancho. It is also unclear exactly where he was born: some accounts say Grande, others San Juan del Rio, and others Durango. Not only this, but his parentage is also the subject of some debate: some believe him to have been the illegitimate son of a wealthy landowner or 'hacendado', Luis Ferman Gurrola, and a maid named Micaela Arambula de Arango, while others contest this theory.

Whatever the truth, there is no doubt that Villa grew up in a poor peasant family, experiencing all the hardships of life at the bottom of the heap. At the age of fifteen, his father died, and he was forced to work the land as a sharecropper to support his widowed mother and his siblings. The following year, he returned home one day to find his twelve-year-old sister being raped by a 'hacendado', or local rancher. He grabbed a gun and shot the man, killing him dead. Fearing for his life, Villa went on the run, hiding in the hills and living as a fugitive. In order to conceal his identity, he adopted the name Francisco Villa.

A 'Robin Hood' figure

By the age of twenty, Villa had become a fully fledged outlaw, and had begun to gravitate towards the city of Chihuahua. He worked from time to time as a miner in Parral, near Chihuahua, and also supplemented his income by cattle rustling, selling the stolen cattle in the markets of the city. (When he eventually became a hero of the Mexican Revolution, his official biography, disseminated by the government, listed his occupation at this time as 'wholesale meat seller'.) Villa then found work in a mine at Santa Eulalia, not far from Chihuahua. However, he quickly tired of the hard labour and low pay, and instead took to robbing banks, thus becoming a wanted man, not only for murder and cattle rustling, but also for robbery.

At the turn of the twentieth century, Pancho Villa had established a colony of bandits in the Sierra mountains, and was sharing the rewards of his escapades with the local population. As a result of this, he became known as something of a Robin Hood figure in the area, not only for his generosity and commitment to helping the poor, but also for the cunning way in which he and his men constantly evaded capture by the authorities. His reputation was aided by the fact that the government of the day, led by Porfirio Diaz, was extremely unpopular, exacting oppressive taxes from poverty-stricken rural workers, and using the money to line their own pockets. The corruption of the authorities was well known throughout the country, so much so that it was considered morally right to obstruct them in any way possible; thus Villa's aim of stealing from the rich to give to the poor made him a hero among the peasants of Mexico. The fact that he was a charismatic individual, by all accounts charming, intelligent and inspiring, also helped to establish his role as a leader of the people.

Bandits and revolutionaries

In 1910, there was an uprising against the Diaz government, known as the Porfiriato, led by Francisco Madero, who was from a middle-class background. When Villa and his men came down from the hills to support Madero, the revolution immediately gained the support of the peasants. Overnight, the 'bandidos' became revolutionaries, and were able to recruit thousands of peasants to their cause, forming a large people's army. Villa's magnetic personality also drew in many Americans, some of whom became captains in the revolutionary army – indeed, there

was one squadron in the army that was entirely composed of American soldiers.

Madero's forces managed to overthrow Diaz and his government, but their victory did not last long. Madero himself was assassinated by reactionary forces and the new regime collapsed. For many years, Mexico was in chaos, without a proper government. In 1913, a new dictatorship, under the leadership of Victoriano Huerta, came into being. However, Villa still remained in control of his peasant army, and now formed a resistance movement, together with other revolutionary leaders such as Venustiano Carranza and Alvaro Obregon. By this time, Villa's fame had spread to the USA, where his status as a folk hero and leader of a revolutionary army made him an object of fascination to the media there, not only in newspapers but in Hollywood films as well.

'The Butcher'

Huerta's new government failed to control Villa, who ruled independently over Chihuahua and the northern part of Mexico as though he were a warring baron in medieval times. Villa and his men made constant raids on the local 'hacendados' or landowners, forcing them to give up their extensive lands, and handing them over to the widows and orphan children of his soldiers who had died in battle. There were rumours of wild, joyous parties at the army camps, where Villa was known to dance all night during 'fiestas' – although he was not a drinker. (Indeed, when he met fellow revolutionary Emiliano Zapata in 1914, before capturing Mexico City, and drank a toast of brandy with him, he was said to

Guard of honour: Pancho Villa and US general Hugh Scott exit together after a conference held during the revolution

have coughed and gagged on it.)

Villa's reputation grew as his power increased in the north. As a keen swimmer and runner, he kept himself in good physical shape and was apparently very attractive to women (by the time he died, he was thought to have married twenty-six times). At the same time, however glamorous his image may have seemed, in reality his regime was a very lawless, violent one. Merchants and shopkeepers who refused to do business with him using the army's banknotes, which they issued themselves, were summarily shot. There were constant executions,

usually at Villa's passing whim, and the dirty work was always left to his right-hand man Rodolfo Fierro. Fierro's savagery earned him the nickname 'El Carnicero', meaning 'The Butcher', and many lived in fear of crossing him.

A wild goose chase

It was not long before the revolutionary leaders, Villa, Carranza and Obregon, began to fall out, arguing with each other over who should take control of the leadership. When Carranza gained the support of the US government, Villa hit back by raiding border towns such as Columbus, New Mexico. His soldiers' violent behaviour made him unpopular with the Americans, who now began to see the sordid reality behind the swashbuckling image of the folk hero. At the same time, Villa's popularity among Mexicans, many of whom were deeply anti-American, began to increase, and he was seen as a hero who was finally seeking revenge for centuries of oppression by their more powerful neighbour.

Over the next few years, Villa became famous for standing up to the United States government, who failed to subdue his soldiers in the North. Each time the US army attacked, he managed to repulse them, leading them on a wild goose chase around the harsh northern territory for months on end. However, when Carranza and Obregon combined their armies against Villa's, attacking his army from within the country, nothing could prevent his eventual defeat. He eventually surrendered to the new government, and retired to Durango, where he lived until 1923, receiving a general's salary from the state.

Ambushed and shot

For reasons that still remain unclear, Villa was ambushed and shot while returning in his car from a visit to a bank in Parral, Chihuahua, on 20 July 1923. Some believe that the assassination of the former revolutionary leader was a government plot, because the assassins were never caught and brought to justice. Three years after his burial, grave robbers dug up his corpse and decapitated it, stealing the head. To date, his skull has not been found.

One theory as to the idea that the Mexican government, supported by the Americans, was behind Villa's assassination suggests that it was done in retaliation for his earlier involvement with anti-American foreign powers. The Germans had apparently supported Villa because they wanted to destabilize America, thus preventing its entry into World War One. At the time, there were other indications that Germany wanted to form an alliance with Mexico against the United States, as evidenced by the Zimmerman Telegram, a telegram written in code from the German foreign secretary, Arthur Zimmerman, to the German ambassador to Mexico, Heinrich von Eckardt. The telegram was intercepted, and it was found that Zimmerman had asked the ambassador to approach the Mexican government with an offer of alliance with Germany against the US.

Today, no one knows just how much Villa knew about this plan, but it seems possible that he could have been involved. Throughout his career, Villa had made alliances with whoever would best advance his cause, in a way that was regarded in some quarters as opportunistic, and in others as pragmatic. But whether the authorities would have reacted, years later, by having him assassinated for this involvement remains questionable.

Whatever the truth of the matter, Villa remains a legendary figure in Mexico, and his reputation as the one Mexican who managed not only to defend his country against Americans, but also to make incursions into American territory, has ensured that his fame will live on.

Pancho Villa with his fellow fighters – his regime turned out to be somewhat violent and lawless

HUEY P. LONG

The assassination of Huey P. Long, a powerful southern politician who was shot to death on 10 September 1935, is still a matter of historical controversy. His assassin was reported to be Carl Weiss, a well-known surgeon in Louisiana. However, some believe that although Weiss shot Long, he did not actually cause his death. According to this theory, Long was accidentally shot by a bodyguard.

The rise of 'The Kingfish'

Huey P. Long was born into a poor southern family in Winnfield, Louisiana, in 1893. He later wrote that when he was sixteen years old, he gained a scholarship to Louisiana State University, but his parents, with five other children, were unable to afford books and living expenses for him to go there. Instead, he found work as a travelling sales-man. He did well, and soon was able to stay in the best hotels, tasting the good life for the first time. He got his university education, studying law at Tulane University, New Orleans, in 1914. A brilliant student, he finished the course in record time, and by the time he was twenty-one was a practising lawyer. He soon began to build a reputation for himself as a defender of poor people's rights. He also joined the Democratic Party, and became known as a champion of the left, attacking the authorities for failing to tax the rich and give benefits to the poor. As chairman of the Public Services Commission, he worked to lower prices for gas, electricity, telephone and transport

services. In 1928, he ran as a candidate for the office of Governor of Louisiana, on a manifesto that emphasized the importance of education for all. This was a major concern in the state, since it had the highest rate of illiteracy in America. He also felt that rich companies and corporations, especially those that supplied basic utilities to the public, were over-privileged and should be held accountable for their activities. His opinions chimed with public sentiment, and he won the election with a landslide majority.

Long's adoption of the campaign slogan 'Every man a king, but no one wears a crown' led to his nickname, 'The Kingfish'. The nickname also came from a popular character in a radio show at the time, *Amos 'n' Andy*. According to Long, the nickname meant, 'I'm a small fish here in Washington, but I'm the Kingfish to the folks down in Louisiana'. Among the sober politicians, Long cut a flamboyant character, and took to wearing a white linen suit, which became his trademark.

Charges of bribery

As Governor, Long continued his campaign to democratize public bodies, and put his own supporters in important municipal positions, so that many began to criticize him for running the state in an authoritarian manner. His governorship of Louisiana was scrutinized by the IRS, and in 1929 he was impeached on charges of bribery and misconduct. However, the Senate did not convict him, failing by a narrow margin to get the requisite number of votes. Whether or not the claim was true, it was certainly the

'Every man a king but no one wears a crown' – Senator Huey Long on the campaign trail in Arkansas during August 1932

case that Long often circumvented the law to get the results he wanted – something that proved very effective in making reforms, but which made him many enemies at all levels of the political spectrum.

Long's barnstorming approach meant that some long-overdue reforms were made quickly, particularly in the area of education, where more money was spent on the state university, on school books, on night-school courses to combat adult illiteracy, on new schools and so on. In addition, Long made tremendous improvements in the road network, taxing the large corporations and businesses to pay for the work. In this way, he made himself very unpopular with the rich and powerful businessmen in the state, who tried to throw him out of office, accusing him of embezzling state funds. They were unsuccessful, and Long's career continued to thrive, until finally he was elected to the Senate. As a Senate member he made constant attacks on President Hoover's handling of the national economy in the period of the Depression.

Next, Long took on the cause of Hattie Caraway who, with his help, became the first woman to be elected to Congress. He also backed Franklin D. Roosevelt, who was campaigning for president of the United States. Once Roosevelt was in office, however, he became disillusioned with the new regime, and attacked the government for failing to help the poor. Although not a socialist, he was extremely critical of the system of inherited wealth, which excluded most Americans from positions of power, and felt that the government should pass legislation and impose taxes so that the situation was more fairly balanced. Accordingly, he launched his Share Our Wealth Society, which campaigned for legislation that would limit large personal fortunes by levying a tax of one per cent for incomes over a million, rising to two per cent for the third million, and so on. He also suggested that the government confiscate all inherited fortunes of over a million. He felt that the money should be used to redistribute wealth among the population, guaranteeing a level of subsistence for the poorest families, subsidizing a minimum income for all, and improving education and health facilities. He was convinced that, if the government did not confront the problems of inequality, there would be revolution; indeed, he saw his plan as an alternative to revolution, saying, 'We haven't a Communist or Socialist in Louisiana. Huey P. Long is the greatest enemy that the Communists and Socialists have to deal with.'

'Coffee blood'

In an era when the Great Depression was making the lives of ordinary people a misery, fragmenting families and communities across the United States, Long's radical ideas proved popular, not only with ordinary citizens, but with politicians as well. However, he also had many enemies, particularly when he began to organize a campaign group to run against Roosevelt in the upcoming election of 1936. Not only were there many attempts to discredit him on a personal level – for example, one story alleged that he was an alcoholic, while another suggested that he had taken bribes

Portrait of a killer? Dr Carl Weiss, a Baton Rouge physician, photographed in his office not long before the assassination

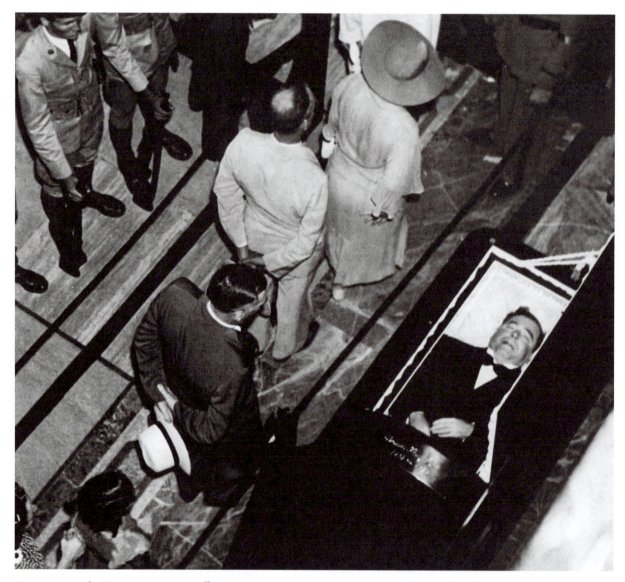

Mourners pass by Huey Long's open coffin in Louisiana – more than 100,000 people attended the funeral, most of them poor

while in office – but there was also a plot to assassinate him. This was uncovered by police, but from then on, Long went everywhere accompanied by bodyguards.

In August 1935, Long announced that he would put himself up as a candidate for the presidency, against Roosevelt. Although he had many supporters, there were also those who thought he was ruthless, and would stop at nothing to achieve his ends. This seems to have been borne out in his fight with a local judge, Benjamin Pavy, that was to lead to his

death. Long ran an election campaign against Pavy in St Landry Parish, but was unable to unseat his rival. To get his own back, he arranged for two of Judge Pavy's daughters, both teachers, to be sacked from their jobs. He also warned Pavy that he would make it known that the family had what he called 'coffee blood', meaning that a black person had been a member of the family. In the racist South, this was a potentially damaging revelation, of course, and the family was horrified at Long's threats.

'Don't let me die'

Carl Weiss, a well-known ear, nose and throat surgeon in Louisiana, was married to Judge Pavy's daughter. When he heard the rumour that his wife was mixed race, he became furious, and paid a visit to Long in the Capitol Building. He waited until Long emerged from the governor's office, and then pulled out a gun and shot him, hitting his victim in the stomach. Long's bodyguards then shot Weiss, who died immediately. During the fight, one of the bullets fired at Weiss also hit Long in the spine.

Long was rushed to hospital, and at first it was thought he would survive. He had an emergency operation to repair the damage, but no one realized that a bullet had hit him in the kidney. His condition deteriorated, until on 10 September 1935, he died. His sister Lucille reported that his final words were: 'Don't let me die, I have got so much to do.'

After the death of Long and that of his assassin, there was much speculation as to what had actually happened. According to some reports, one of the bullets meant for Weiss, fired by a bodyguard, had actually ricocheted off a pillar in the hallway and gone into Long's body, causing his eventual death. The marks where the bullet nicked the pillar are still visible in the hallway to this day. Others alleged that Weiss was not armed, and had only hit Long as he walked along the corridor. When Long went into hospital for surgery, it was noted that he had a bruised lip, which may have been the result of a fracas with Weiss. According to this version of the story, Weiss had not meant to kill Long, but simply to punch him, and therefore, Long's bodyguards, who had

opened fire on Weiss, were entirely responsible for their boss's demise.

There was also a great deal of speculation as to Weiss's motivation. The story about his wife was one reason for him to seek revenge on Long, but there was also a theory that Weiss had visited Germany in 1935 and seen parallels between the rise of Adolf Hitler in Germany and that of Huey P. Long in the USA. According to this theory, Weiss saw Long as a demagogue, and was afraid that Long's 'Share the Wealth' campaign was a brand of national socialism, or Nazi ideology, under another name. Another theory is that the assassination was arranged by powerful elements in the political world to prevent Long from winning the presidential campaign against Roosevelt. Whatever the truth of the matter, the assassination of Huey P. Long, known as 'The Kingfish', brought to an end one of the most colourful, and – many would argue – the most progressive administrations in the history of the South.

CZAR ALEXANDER II OF RUSSIA

One of the most shocking assassinations of history was that of Alexander II, who was czar of Russia from 1855 until his death in 1881. Alexander II was in some ways one of the more liberal monarchs of Russia, and it was under his regime that the emancipation of the serfs took place. However, his reforms did not go far enough, and poverty was still a huge problem throughout Russia, so much so that a revolutionary fervour gripped the

Alexander II, Czar of Russia, normally travelled with two trains, one to test the safety of the tracks, the other to carry him

country. There were several attempts on Czar Alexander's life, and by the time he died, his security forces were on high alert. However, despite their caution, the czar was eventually killed in a bomb attack that not only blew him apart, but also killed his assassin, and twenty others, as well as injuring many more. According to onlookers, the scene of the crime was a bloodbath, the snow turning red as the wounded bled to death, with fragments of human flesh hanging from the trees and lamp posts in the street.

Ironically, the assassination of the czar only led to worse problems in Russia, as his successor Alexander III was profoundly reactionary, and became so unpopular that by the end of his reign he was virtually a prisoner in his own palace. By the time his son Nicholas II came to the throne, repression had reached such a level that there was a massive revolution, led by the Bosheviks, and Nicholas was brutally assassinated, along with his whole family. Thus, Alexander's assassination was the beginning of the end for the czars of Russia, whose despotic rule came to an end with the revolution of 1917.

Brutal repression

Alexander II Nikolaevitch was born on 17 April 1818, the eldest son of Czar Nicholas I of Russia. As a boy, he was kind-hearted and even-tempered, to the disappointment of his father, who wished that he would display virtues more suited to a military leader. The young Alexander showed little interest in military affairs or politics, and seemed disinclined to change the status quo, which

was one of extreme inequalities between rich and poor, together with brutal repression and censorship of any criticism about the government of the day.

In 1841, Alexander married Princess Marie of Hesse, with whom he had six children. His wife later died, and he married his mistress, Princess Catherine Dolgoruki, who was mother to four more children. When his father died, Alexander became czar, and spent his initial years in power overseeing the Crimean War. When this was over, he devoted himself to reforms that were desperately needed to put the country back on an equal footing with other European powers. Without relinquishing his autocratic powers, he began to pass laws to help modernize industry and commerce, and planned the creation of an infrastructure of railways across the country. He also realized, unlike his predecessors, that Russia could not advance any further under the system of serfdom, by which peasants were tied to the land with very few rights of their own. Accordingly, he passed laws to emancipate the serfs, and make them independent; however, he also imposed heavy taxation on them, so they were not a great deal better off in the long run. In addition, the government brutally suppressed the January Uprising of 1863, killing and deporting thousands of Poles. Criticism of the regime grew stronger, until Alexander felt forced to adopt repressive new measures, including the banning of minority languages in some parts of the country. Not surprisingly, this led to a great deal of unrest and bitterness, and it was not long before Alexander and his government realized that their days were numbered.

There were several attempts on the life of the czar: on one occasion a student threw a bomb at his passing carriage

Misfired shots

There were several assassination attempts on the czar. In 1866, Dmitry Karakozov, a student, arrived in St Petersburg with the intention of assassinating Alexander. On 4 April, he went to the gates of the Summer Garden, drew his gun, and was about to shoot the czar when a bystander, Osip Komissarov, prevented him by jostling his elbow. Some argue that Komissarov, a peasant who had come to work in St Petersburg as a hatter's apprentice, intervened because he loved the czar, while others allege it was an accident, or perhaps that it never happened at all. Whatever the truth, Karakozov tried to make a run for it, but was arrested. He was later hanged in public in St Petersburg. Komissarov, on the other hand, was rewarded with a title and money, but went on to embarrass the government with his uncouth behaviour, and was sent to live out of town. The czar commissioned a new gate for the city, to commemorate his escape from death.

The next attempt came on the morning of 20 April 1879, when a student, Alexander Soloviev, walked towards the czar holding a gun. The czar quickly retreated, and Soloviev fired at him. There were five shots, but miraculously, all of them missed the target. Soloviev was arrested and hanged the following month.

Also in 1879, a group of radicals called 'Will of the People' attempted to blow up a train in which the czar was travelling. The attempt failed when explosives did not detonate as planned, blowing up a train – but the wrong train. The czar normally travelled with two trains, one to test the safety of the tracks, and one to carry him; but in this case, the first train had been carrying the czar. The plotters were outwitted – but not for long.

In 1880, there was another extraordinary attack. This time, assassins blew up the dining room of the czar's Winter Palace. This was a spectacular attempt, but it too failed, this time because the czar and his family had been late arriving for dinner.

After these terrifying attempts, the czar's advisers were determined to keep him out of harm's way, and arranged for him to cut down on his public appearances. He was also advised to discontinue travelling by railway, and to travel by boat instead, as often as possible. However, Alexander was determined to continue his activities as monarch, and refused to be hemmed in by his security men. He announced that he did not fear death, and pointed out that he had already survived several assassination attempts, and had lived longer than most of his ancestors.

Legs blown off

But his confidence was misplaced, as it turned out. On 1 March 1881, Alexander went to review his troops. A group of radicals were waiting for him, including Andrei Zhelyabov, a brilliant leader who had been born a serf and had educated himself so that he had eventually gained a scholarship from the University of Odessa. With Zhelyabov was his lover, Sophia Perovskaya, also a political activist. The pair had rented a shop along one of the streets the czar and his family were due to ride through, and had pretended to be cheese sellers at the shop in the days running up to the event. In fact, what they had been doing was tunnelling

under the street and planting explosives in a spot where they would blow up the czar's carriage as it passed by. They also positioned four men in the street, all armed with bombs to throw at the czar if the explosion failed.

The police were on Zhelyabov's tail, however, and just before the event took place, they arrested him. Perovskaya was left to manage the attack, but the plan failed when the czar took an unscheduled route. Instead of passing down the street where the explosives were planted, the carriage went another way, which meant that the bomb attackers had to leap into action. The job was left to a nineteen-year-old student, Rysakov, who emerged out of the crowd, dressed as a common peasant. He threw the bomb right at the czar's carriage, damaging the door of the vehicle and rocking it from side to side. However, the czar continued on his way, unhurt, although a boy who was standing in the street was killed. Two of the czar's Cossack escorts, and several horses, were also killed, and some soldiers were also hurt. Rysakov was arrested, taken into police custody, and later executed.

The czar then stopped his carriage and got out to see what was going on. He walked around, offering assistance to those who were wounded. He then turned towards another carriage, determined to travel on and continue the day's scheduled events. However, just as he was doing so, another assassin, Ignaty Grinevitsky, ran towards the czar, throwing a nitroglycerine bomb right at him. This time, there was no escape: the bomb blew up Alexander's legs, and took out one of his eyes. It was clear that the czar was about to die, and Grinevitsky too was fatally wounded. Not only this, but around them, twenty onlookers lay dead, and many more in the crowd were injured.

By now, the dying Alexander knew that his time was up, and managed to order his aides to get him to the palace as quickly as possible so that he could say farewell to his loved ones. An hour later, he died, attended by his family members.

Tyrannical rule

The aftermath of the assassination was a dismal one. Instead of instigating revolution, liberal and left-wing opposition to the regime collapsed. The six main conspirators involved in the assassination plot were tried and found guilty.

All of them were executed. Radicals all over the country went into hiding, disbanding their organizations. Partly as a result of the bloody end to Alexander II's regime, his successor, Alexander III, clamped down on any form of political activism, and proved an extremely repressive monarch, deeply opposed to any kind of reform, and determined to turn the clock back as much as possible in Russia. For over a decade, any kind of opposition to the government was banned, and Russia's social system returned to the backwardness that had characterized it before the reign of Alexander III.

When Alexander III died prematurely in 1894, the hapless Nicholas II took over, and became the last of the czars to rule Russia. He and his entire family were eventually shot by ruthless revolutionaries in the Russian Revolution, bringing to an end the tyrannical rule of the czars of Russia, and ushering in a new, equally turbulent, era of Soviet socialism. Thus Alexander II's brutal assassination proved the first of a long line of violent actions whereby the members of the Romanov dynasty lost their place as rulers of the Russian empire.

RASPUTIN

Grigori Yefimovich Rasputin has gone down in history as one of the most infamous characters of all time. His death, like his life, was highly dramatic. Alarmed by his corrupting influence on the Russian royal family, a group of assassins tried to kill him, but he displayed an almost supernatural ability to survive poisoning, gun shot wounds and drowning. Eventually, this great bear of a man met his end, terrifying those around him with his extraordinary – though not, in the end, superhuman – powers. He left a lasting legacy, not so much because of his direct influence in politics, but because he played an important part in undermining the reputation of the Romanov family, who became the last of Russia's monarchs to hold power before the revolution of 1917.

The mad monk

Nobody knows exactly when Rasputin was born, but it was thought to be some time around 1870. He grew up in a small Siberian village called Pokrovskoye, but as a young man left home to wander the country as a 'staret' or 'holy man'. He had no formal education and was illiterate. He spent several months in a monastery, joining the Khlysty, a secret sect that had broken off from the Russian Orthodox church. The sect was known to preach asceticism as a way of attaining spiritual ecstasy, in particular emphasizing flagellation, but its members were rumoured to indulge in mass orgies.

Rasputin married and fathered several children, but continued his pilgrimages around the country, proclaiming himself to be a psychic and faith healer. He eventually arrived in St Petersburg where the czar and czarina asked him for help to cure their son, Alexei, of haemophilia. Although he was unable to heal the boy completely, Rasputin had an uncanny knack of easing his distressing bleeding, so much so that the czarina came to rely on him for help, believing him to have divine powers. Meanwhile, the ill-kempt 'mad monk', as Rasputin now became known, scandalised St Petersburg society by sleeping with scores of women from aristocrats to common whores, and drinking to excess. (There were even rumours that he was having a sexual relationship with the czarina, although there is very little evidence to suggest that this was actually the case.)

The man they couldn't kill

Rasputin was also thought to have a strong political influence over the czar, as well as the czarina, helping to determine key government appointments. It was this that began to worry the Russian nobility, as well as the British government and other European nations. Not surprisingly, the Romanovs' new friend brought the family into disrepute, and they soon became very unpopular, both at home and abroad.

Eventually a group of young nobles, Prince Felix Yusopov, Vladimir Purishkevich, and Grand Duke Dmitri Pavlovitch Romanov, a cousin of the czar's, took it upon themselves to assassinate Rasputin, hoping that in this way they could rid the royal family of the stain on their reputation. On the night of 29 December 1916, Prince Felix invited Rasputin to his palace on the Moika Canal, to meet his beautiful wife Irina, a niece of the czar's. Yusopov had for some time cultivated a friendship with Rasputin, and may well have had some personal, as well as political, reason to kill him. At the palace, Rasputin was plied with cakes and wine. The food and drink was contaminated with cyanide, so Yusopov was waiting for him to drop dead, but was amazed to find that the poisoning seemed to have little effect on his guest. In a panic, Yusopov shot Rasputin, who staggered out into the courtyard, wounded and bleeding. There, the other conspirators, who were preparing to leave the palace, shot him again, but he amazed them too by remaining alive. Finally, the group picked him up and took him to the river, pushing his body through a hole in the ice, where he is thought to have moved about for a short while before dying. Several days later, the czarina ordered the body to be retrieved from the river for burial.

The final bullet

There are several theories as to why Rasputin took so long to die from poisoning. It is possible that Rasputin never actually swallowed the poison, or that if he did, it was not effective. It may have been that the sugar in the pastries and wine cancelled the effect of the cyanide, or that as Rasputin was a

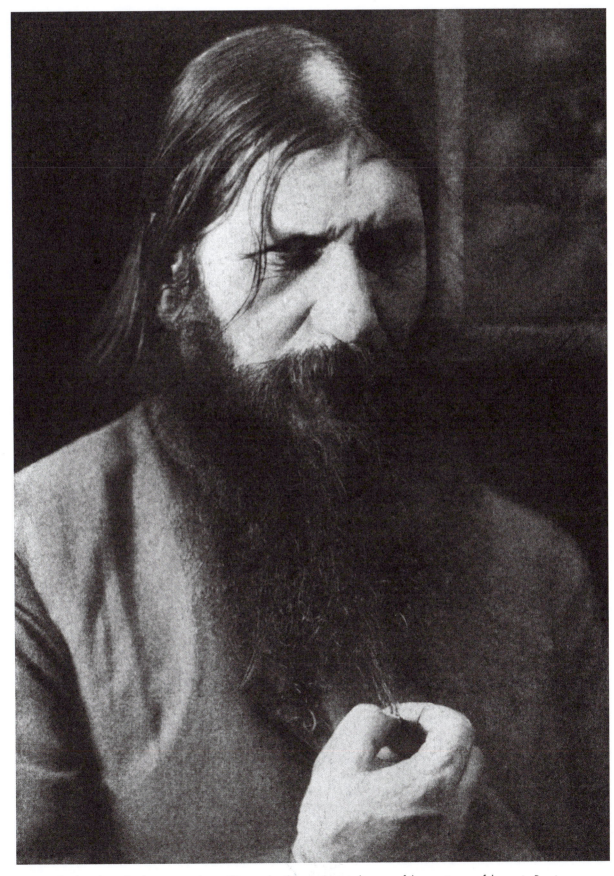

Rasputin had no formal education and was illiterate but he grew up to be one of the most powerful men in Russia

Friends in high places: Rasputin, flanked by Captain von Lohman and Prince Poutiatine (rt), wielded great political influence

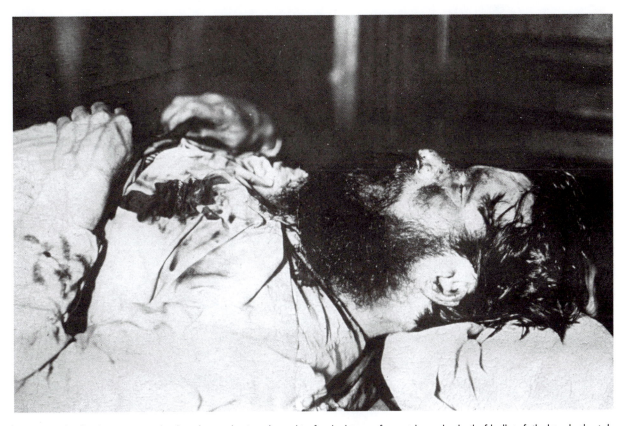

Rasputin's body: the assassins had to drown the 'mad monk' after lashings of cyanide and a hail of bullets failed to do the job

heavy drinker, the chemical make-up of his digestive system protected him from being poisoned. Some accounts also suggest that one of the nobles may have been double-crossing his co-conspirators, and trying to prevent the murder from taking place.

Many commentators have come up with various theories to explain why Rasputin did not immediately die of his gunshot wounds. It appears that he may have been shot in places such as the lung and liver, which are not immediately fatal and so did not instantly cause his death.

New evidence has recently come to light that a British secret service agent may also have been involved in the shooting. The theory is that the British were worried about Rasputin's influence over the German-born czarina at the time of World War One, and

sent an assassin to Russia to kill him. To cover up British involvement, the agent secretly participated in the assassination by Prince Yusopov and his friends.

Accordingly, the agent hid in a bush while Yusopov's group were carrying out the murder, and shot Rasputin in the head with a pistol when he tried to escape – it is in fact possible that it was the British agent's bullet that finally brought the monk's life to an end.

Today, Rasputin's life and death continues to be the subject of much speculation and interest. Rasputin apparently knew he was about to be assassinated, and is said to have claimed, on the night of his murder, that if the deed was carried out by nobles, Russia would undergo bloody warfare for many years. His prediction came true, as the events of the Russian Revolution went on to show.

CHAPTER THREE

STABBED IN THE BACK

The assassination of any important figure, whether admirable or not, is always shocking. In the case of those who have been murdered by those they thought of as friends, colleagues or followers, it is particularly so.

In this chapter we explore one of the most infamous assassinations of all time – the stabbing of Julius Caesar as he fell at the feet of the statue of Pompey, a previous Roman emperor, at the Senate in Rome. At the time of his death, Caesar had achieved immense power at the head of the great Roman republic, and there were signs that he considered himself to be almost a god among men, crowning himself in glory and holding huge celebrations to mark his reign. It was perhaps this autocratic behaviour that made him such a threat to his colleagues, who gathered together in a group of sixty, and plotted to kill him in the most vicious way. Central to the plot was Marcus Brutus, who was widely regarded as a virtuous man, and whom some believed to be the son of Caesar (Caesar had once been the lover of Brutus' mother Servilia). On the fatal day of his death, Caesar ignored warnings and entered the Senate, only to be surrounded by the conspirators, who crowded around him and overpowered him, stabbing him repeatedly. While he was dying, Caesar could see all of the men whom he had once

regarded as his friends, including Brutus, so that he died in the most ignominious way, knowing that he had been betrayed by his own son.

The same sense of shock pervades our description of the assassination of Thomas Becket, the Archbishop of Canterbury who had been a close friend of the king of England, Henry II, in the twelfth century. Alarmed at Becket's increasing power as the head of the church, often in conflict with the state, Henry sent four knights to murder his former friend. They chased him into Canterbury Cathedral and stabbed him to death at the altar, in an act that horrified the whole of Christendom and went down in history as one of the most shameful betrayals of all time.

Equally horrifying are the deaths of Leon Trotsky, stabbed to death with an ice pick in the skull, and Jean-Paul Marat, murdered in his bath by a knife-wielding young woman. In both cases, the victims were killed by people they thought to be followers. Ramon Mercader, Trotsky's assassin, was a Stalinist secret agent who gained Trotsky's trust by pretending to be an aspiring political journalist and asking him for advice on his writing. In a similar way, Marat's assassin Charlotte Corday gained entry to his private quarters by pretending to be a political follower. Interestingly, Corday is the only female assassin listed here who successfully murdered her victim; the other woman is would-be assassin Valerie Solanas, who tried but failed to kill Andy Warhol (her attempt is described in the last chapter, *Near Misses)*.

Also described here is the fascinating case of Georgi Markov, the Bulgarian dissident who defected to Britain and broadcast to his compatriots there from BBC radio in London. He was bitterly opposed to the oppressive regime in Bulgaria, and was outspoken about his views. One day, on a lunch break, he took a stroll over Waterloo Bridge, and was stabbed with a poisoned umbrella spike by a secret service agent from his homeland, in an action worthy of a spy thriller.

THOMAS BECKET

The assassination of Thomas Becket, often known as Thomas à Becket, is one of the most notorious events of medieval history. Once a friend and advisor of King Henry II of England, he had fallen out of favour, but there are different theories as to why the killing took place. Whatever the truth, the brutal murder of the highest religious figure in the land profoundly shocked the people of Europe, at a time when the Christian religion was extremely important in even the lowest-born person's life.

Thomas Becket was born in 1118 in London, England, to Gilbert of Thierceville, Normandy, France, and his wife Rosea. Thierceville was a wealthy merchant with political connections. (The name 'Becket' was later incorrectly changed to 'à Becket',

perhaps signifying that there were those in England who wished to consider Thomas Becket as a Frenchman and a foreigner, rather than a true-born Englishman, but the exact reason for this change remains somewhat mysterious.)

Allegiance to the king

Becket had a privileged childhood, learning to ride, hunt and joust, and for his education attended Merton Priory in England, where he studied law, among other things. He continued his studies overseas, in Paris, Bologna and Auxerre. He was then sent to work for Theobold, the archbishop of Canterbury, who was head of the English church. Becket impressed the archbishop with his charm, intelligence and administrative ability, and quickly rose in the archbishop's service to become archdeacon of Canterbury.

In 1154, Becket met the new king of England, Henry II. The two of them got on well, and became friends. Becket later became lord chancellor to the king. During this time, in the many struggles for power between the church and the state, Becket was a staunch ally of the king, so much so that when Theobold died in 1161, the king immediately made Becket archbishop of Canterbury.

This was despite the fact that Becket was not an ordained priest – but the king solved this problem by ordaining him first as a priest, then as a bishop, and then as archbishop of Canterbury – all in a matter of days. The king hoped that, by making his friend Becket the most important religious leader in the land, he would

Becket and Henry II in close council. Political rivalries may have meant the knights acted more swiftly than they should have

The king's four knights hacked Thomas Becket to pieces in full view of the congregation at Canterbury Cathedral

ensure that the church remained on the side of the monarchy.

However, once Becket became archbishop, King Henry began to realize he had made a mistake. Having been a merry, worldly companion to the king, Becket now became serious and monastic, adopting simple robes and solemnly attending to his religious duties. (Later, it was found that, in keeping with his newly adopted puritanical spirit, he wore a hair shirt under his clothes.)

He also refused to be at the king's beck and call any longer, and worked to ensure that the church had its own sphere of influence, separate from that of the crown. For example, the king wanted to try priests who had committed criminal offences in the crown courts; Becket argued that they should be tried by religious authorities in the church's own courts.

Forced into exile

Often, when clerics were tried in the church court, they received light sentences or were acquitted. This is what happened in 1163, when a priest accused of murder was let off, much to the dismay of the public, who called for a fairer trial.

King Henry began to increase pressure for the church to hand over their legal powers to the state, but Becket resisted, refusing to agree to this. Eventually, the quarrels between the two men escalated, and Becket was forced into exile in France, where he remained for six years.

When he returned, it soon became clear that relations between the king and Becket had not improved. The quarrels continued, this time over the matter of the Bishops of London, whom Becket had excommunicated for siding with the king. King Henry wanted Becket to pardon the bishops, but Becket refused. Henry became more and more infuriated with Becket for standing up to him, and in the end was reported to shout, 'What cowards have I brought to my court, who care nothing for allegiance to their lord? Will no one rid me of this meddlesome priest?' (Other reports attest that he shouted 'lowborn' rather than 'meddlesome', but there is no doubt that he expressed his frustration with Becket in no uncertain terms.)

Skull split

As always at the court, there were knights who wanted to curry favour with the king, and on hearing this, four of them decided to travel to Canterbury to seek out Becket and 'rid' the king of him. The knights, William Tracy, Hugh de Morville, Reginald Fitzurse and Richard Briton, took with them a posse of armed soldiers. They arrived on 29 December and accosted him, at which point he fled to Canterbury Cathedral where a service was taking place. There, the knights followed him up to the altar, and delivered an ultimatum, that he should withdraw the excommunications. He refused, and the knights pulled out their swords. Fitzurse attacked first, slashing Becket with his sword. The four knights hacked Becket to pieces, splitting his skull in the process, right in front of the altar in God's house, in full view of the congregation.

The assassination was witnessed by Edward Grim, a monk, who was standing near the altar when the crime occurred. He told how the knights called on Becket to absolve the excommunicated individuals, and how Becket claimed that they had done nothing to deserve absolution, and that he would not pardon them. Then, according to Grim, the knights called out that he deserved to die, and drew their swords. Becket told them that they were behaving like madmen, and began to pray as Reginald Fitzurse lunged at him, wounding him. Next, one of the knights cut the top of his head at the crown, and in the fight that ensued Grim himself was wounded. Becket received more blows and continued to pray, until he was finally silenced. The knights then fled from the cathedral.

A sacrilegious act

Besides being a horrifyingly brutal murder, this was also a sacrilegious act, which appalled Christians throughout Europe. Becket was quickly made a saint, and King Henry vilified for the cold-blooded murder of the most important religious leader in England. Henry, for his part, claimed that he had merely spoken in anger, and had not meant his remark to be taken seriously. Such was the public outcry at the murder, however, that four years later, the king was forced to do penance for the crime. He was made to walk barefoot through the streets of Canterbury, wearing a pilgrim's gown, and underneath it a hair shirt, until he came to Becket's tomb in the Cathedral, where he knelt down, confessed, and asked the dead man's pardon. He then bared his back and was lashed with branches by eighty monks, so that his skin was covered in welts.

It seems that, in death, Thomas Becket

finally had his revenge on King Henry II – a little too late, however, to take pleasure in it.

LEON TROTSKY

The assassination of Leon Davidovitch Trotsky is one of the most dramatic murders in history. He was savagely attacked at his house in Coyoacan, Mexico, by a Soviet agent, Ramon Mercader. Mercader hid an ice pick in his coat, then pulled it out while Trotsky was reading and dealt him a massive blow on the head, mortally wounding him. Bleeding profusely, Trotsky struggled with his attacker, but eventually collapsed and died. Although Trotsky had been one of the major figures of the Russian Revolution, he was never honoured in his home country; however, his theory of communism, and his implacable opposition to Stalinism, continue to this day to be significant contributions to political thought. His life had been full of drama, adventure, activity and passion; and as he lived, so he died.

The passionate revolutionary

Trotsky was born Leon Bronstein on 7 November 1879 in the tiny village of Yanovka in the Ukraine. (It has been noted that, according to the ancient Julian calendar, his birth date fell on 26 October, the same day that the Russian Revolution of 1917 broke out.) His father was a farmer who was unable to read or write, but the family were quite wealthy so the young Trotsky was sent to Odessa to be educated. As a young man, he studied mathematics at university, but spent most of his time writing

Bolshevik leader Leon Trotsky, one of the major figures of the Russian Revolution, was killed with an ice pick by a Soviet agent

8 November 1921: Red Square is packed with thousands of hushed soldiers and citizens listening to Leon Trotsky's words

Marxist pamphlets under the name 'Lvov', until he was arrested and jailed. So began his first spell in prison, during which time he studied philosophy and married a comrade, Aleksandra Sokolvskaya. He was then sent to Siberia, where he remained in exile for four years before escaping to join fellow Russian revolutionaries such as Lenin, Plekhanov and Martov in London. It was at this time that he acquired the name 'Trotsky', which was the name on his stolen passport.

At the time of the outbreak of the Russian Revolution in 1917, Trotsky was living as an exile in New York. He managed to make his way back to his homeland, and became part of the new government of Lenin and his Bolshevik party. He formed and led the new government's military force, the Red Army, which went on to brutally suppress the Kronstadt Rebellion, an uprising of working people that took place in 1921. This was a crucial event in the history of the USSR, and ushered in a new phase of repressive state bureacracy that was to continue throughout most of the twentieth century.

Exiled once more

When Lenin became ill and died in 1924, a bitter power struggle, both ideological and personal, took place between Trotsky and Joseph Stalin. Stalin triumphed; Trotsky was expelled from the party, and once more found himself in exile. He travelled around Europe and then went to live in Mexico, where he continued to write about the progress of the revolution, and to agitate against Stalin's increasingly vicious regime. Not surprisingly, Trotsky's activities made him extremely unpopular with Stalin and

Sheer treachery: Trotsky was struck on the back of the skull while helpfully reading an article his assassin had written

the Communist government in the USSR. It was not long before he began to receive visits from the NKVD, the Russian Secret Service, at his home in Coyoacan, Mexico City. In May 1940, assassins conducted a raid on the house, aided by the Mexican painter David Siqueiros, who supported the Stalinist regime. Even though the attackers fired several rounds of bullets at the house, miraculously all the occupants escaped unharmed. A few months later, however, on 20 August, a second attack took place; this time, it was successful.

The fatal ice pick

Having failed to kill Trotsky in a hail of bullets, the agents of the Russian Secret Service now decided on a different plan of action: to hire an assassin who would do the job with an ice pick. They had just the man to carry out the attack: Jaime Ramon Mercader. Mercader's mother, Caridad, had worked as a Soviet agent and Mercader junior had continued the family's line of business, training in Moscow as a saboteur and assassin. Posing as a Canadian, Frank Jacson, Mercader had travelled to Mexico City and had become friendly with members of Trotsky's family and entourage, feigning an interest in politics. Unbeknownst to the Trotskys, 'Jacson' had been involved in the first raid on the family house, but this fact did not emerge until later.

On the fateful day of 20 August, 'Jacson' visited the house, pretending to have revised an article that Trotsky had previously corrected for him. He carried a coat with him, under which he had hidden a steel ice pick, the handle shortened so that it would be easier to conceal. (The 'ice pick' method was well tried and tested by the NKVD, and had been used on several occasions before; it was held to be a quick, easy murder method.) Up the street, his mother Caridad and another agent were waiting in a car for him to make his getaway.

Trotsky had not been very impressed with his new friend's political writings so far, and had told members of his family that he considered 'Jacson' 'light-minded', but out of politeness he agreed to look over the revised article again.

The men went to Trotsky's study, and Trotsky sat down to read the article. As Trotsky bent his head over the paper, 'Jacson' saw his opportunity, picked up the ice pick, and dashed it into Trotsky's skull.

Treated as a hero

Unfortunately, the blow was badly aimed, and although blood gushed from Trotsky's head, he remained alive and extremely vocal for some time. According to Mercader, he let out a blood-curdling yell, which haunted the murderer for the rest of his life, and began to fight with his attacker. Hearing the commotion, Trotsky's bodyguards rushed in from another room. They were always on hand, since by this time Trotsky lived each day in fear of his life. Trotsky, rational to the last, told them not to kill Mercader, saying, 'He has a story to tell.'

A doctor was immediately called, and police surrounded the house. His mother and the other agent, sensing that the plan had failed, escaped. By the time Trotsky's grandson, Seva Volkov, returned home from school, he found a scene of murder and mayhem, with his grandfather lying on the floor covered in blood.

Trotsky was rushed to hospital and died the next day. He put up an extraordinary struggle, remaining conscious for several hours even though the wound to his head was deep. Mercader received a twenty-year jail sentence for murder but did not reveal his true identity. In 1960, he was released,

Julius Caesar was killed by a group of aristocratic rivals at a time when his popularity with the people was at an all-time high

went to Cuba and then to the USSR, where he was treated as a hero. He died in 1978.

JULIUS CAESAR

The assassination of Julius Caesar is one of the most infamous episodes in history. He was killed by a group of aristocratic rivals at a time when his popularity among the common folk of Rome had reached new heights, having returned triumphantly to the republic after successfully defeating his great rival Pompey. As a result of his success in establishing Rome and its empire, Caesar had been made 'dictator for life'. There were also moves to crown him king, which angered many high-ranking figures in the Senate. Sixty members of the Senate, including Marcus Junius Brutus Caepio, supposedly a friend of Caesar's, secretly plotted to kill him, and the murder took place on 15 March ('The Ides of March'), 44BC.

The plot

The conspirators met secretly in each other's houses to plan the attack. It was initially proposed that Caesar should be ambushed and killed while he went on one of his favourite walks, along the 'Sacred Way'; others suggested that he should be pushed over a bridge during the forthcoming elections; yet others thought that the murder should take place during a gladiator show. The final decision was to kill Caesar during a session at the Senate, so that there would be few witnesses. Another advantage of attacking Caesar in the Senate was that weapons could be hidden beneath the togas that Senate members always wore.

Caesar had set the date for the next meeting of the Senate on 15 March, known as 'The Ides of March' in the Roman calendar. Legend has it that he was told by a soothsayer to avoid this date; the soothsayer told him to 'beware the Ides of March', but he ignored this advice and went ahead. As the day approached, rumours began to circulate as to what was going to happen. Some of Caesar's friends asked him to avoid the Senate house, and his wife Calpurnia declared that she had had a vision in a dream which showed that he would be harmed if he went out that day. Caesar himself reportedly felt unwell, and was suffering from dizziness, a condition that occasionally afflicted him. However, he was eventually persuaded to attend the Senate by his trusted friend Brutus, who told him to ignore 'idle gossip' and the advice of his wife, which was merely based on irrational dreams. Brutus pointed out that Caesar would be dishonouring the Senate if he did not go that day.

It was the practice among Roman priests to make sacrifices to the gods on behalf of their rulers, and before Caesar went in to the Senate chamber, he took part in one of these rituals. The priests told him that the omens were bad, whereupon Caesar became impatient with the procedures and left the priests to their work, promising to return later in the day. Frightened by the bad omens, Caesar's friends begged him not to continue to the Senate chamber, but once again Brutus intervened, telling him that his power as dictator was mightier than that of

Julius Caesar was attacked on the steps of the Senate and could not defend himself against so many conspirators

the priests, and taking him by the hand to lead him on to his place of death.

Thirty-five stab wounds

When Caesar entered the Senate chamber, everyone stood up, which was customary as a mark of respect to their leader. A man named Tillius Cimber approached him, pretending that he had come to plead mercy for his brother, who had been exiled. Cimber pulled at Caesar's toga, which irritated Caesar, who pushed him away. At this point, the other conspirators rushed in, taking out their daggers and stabbing at him.

The first to strike was Servilius Casca, who aimed a thrust at Caesar's shoulder, and missed. Casca shouted at his brother, who then drove a sword into Caesar's ribs. Next to strike was Cassius, cutting Caesar's face, and Decimus Brutus, thrusting his dagger into Caesar's side. A couple of the senators, Cassius Longinus and Minucius, managed to hit their co-conspirators, Marcus Brutus and Rubrius, instead of Caesar. All in all it was an incompetent, cowardly attack, with each of the conspirators determined to make their strike. With so many ranged against him, Caesar soon fell down dead, with thirty-five stab wounds on his body. Ironically, he fell at the feet of the statue of Pompey, his old rival.

The conspirators rapidly disappeared and Caesar lay there unconscious for ages, until at last three slaves arrived with a litter to carry him home with one arm dangling down. Oddly enough, given how many wounds he received, only one would have been mortal according to the physician – the second blow to the breast and into his heart.

Why was Caesar killed?

The assassination of Julius Caesar has been the subject of much controversy ever since it happened. According to some commentators, Caesar provoked the members of the Senate by becoming too greedy for power, and assassinating him was their only way of getting rid of him. Caesar's power had grown too all-encompassing: on his return from war, he had proclaimed himself a lifelong dictator, and looked as though he was aiming to crown himself king of Rome some time in the near future. However, other historians point out that this simply was not the case: it can be argued that Caesar was, on the contrary, extremely careful to distance himself from those who wanted to give him too much power. For example, just a month before, at the Feast of Lupercalia, Caesar had publicly rejected the title of king, thrusting off a crown that his supporter, Mark Antony, had tried to place on his head. Far from being hungry for power, Caesar was acutely aware of the danger that too much power might place him in; he knew Senate members were jealous of his popularity among the people, and was clever enough not to alienate his colleagues in the Senate by pandering to the crowd's cravings for a demagogue.

Whatever the truth of the matter, today the assassination of Julius Caesar stands as a powerful symbol of a brave, dignified man bitterly betrayed by those he trusted, especially his close friend Brutus. His last words, according to Shakespeare in the play *Julius Caesar*, were 'Et tu, Brute?' – 'And even you, Brutus?'. (In actual fact, as reported by Suetonius, Caesar said, 'You too, my child?')

JEAN-PAUL MARAT

The assassination of Jean-Paul Marat is one of the most famous events of the French Revolution, and was immortalized by the painter Jacques-Louis David. David had visited the revolutionary leader on the day before he was murdered, and so was able to draw many of the details from memory. Nevertheless, his portrait was an idealized one, in keeping with the spirit of revolutionary fervour at the time.

A brutal demagogue

Jean-Paul Marat, born in 1743, was a doctor and scientist who became a journalist and politician at the time of the French Revolution. For some, he was a great visionary, who was determined to protect the revolution at all costs; for others, he was a violent, brutal demagogue who delighted in his task of beheading those who opposed him. For not only was Marat in favour of guillotining members of the aristocracy, he also denounced those moderate revolutionaries who criticized the revolutionary regime as inhuman and unjust.

For many, Marat's greatest crime was to approve the massacre of over a thousand prisoners, jailed because of their opposition to the revolutionary leaders. Not only men, but also women and children, were sent to the guillotine.

Marat knew that many of the prisoners were, in fact, completely innocent of any crime, but felt that a steady supply of victims was necessary to keep the crowds baying for blood and sympathetic to the revolution.

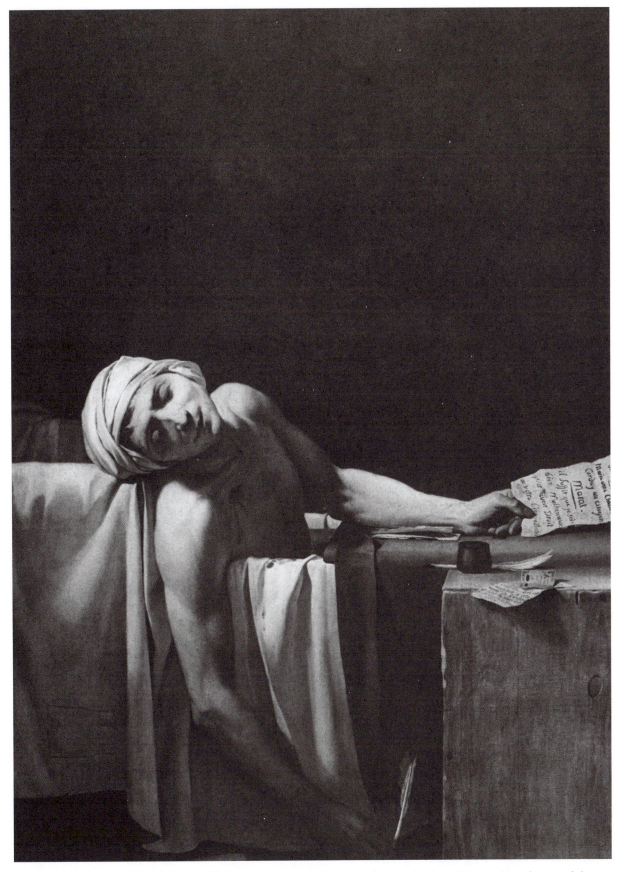

The idealized portrait of Marat: in fact he liked to maintain a steady supply of victims for the guillotine to keep the crowds happy

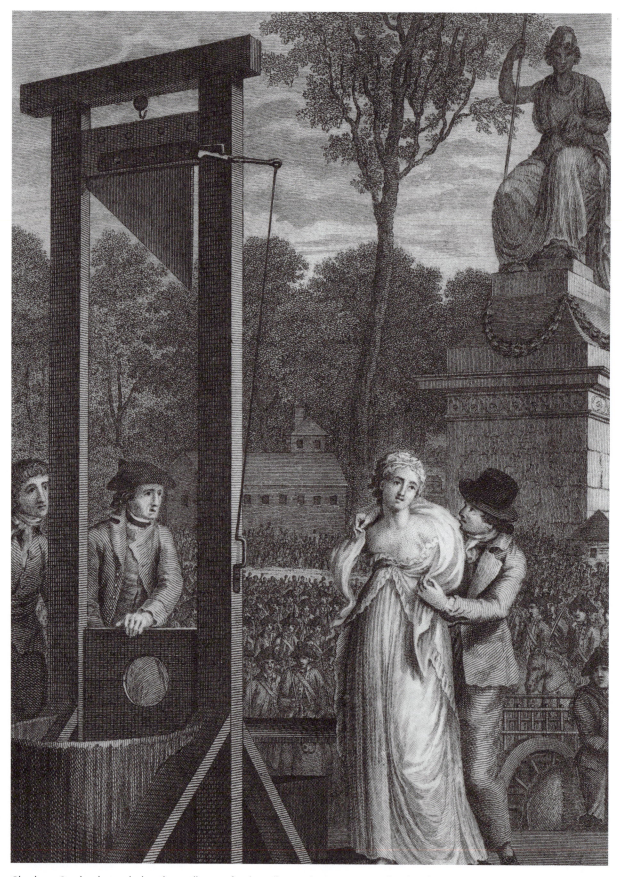

Charlotte Corday being led to the guillotine after brutally murdering Marat with a butcher's knife while he sat in his bath

Accordingly, he established a secret network of spies, to root out those supposedly opposed to the revolution. He also took pleasure in making long lists of those he wished to be put to death. He was one of the principle upholders of the 'reign of terror', in which thousands were slaughtered, turning the French Revolution into a bloodbath that terrified the rest of Europe.

Death lists

Charlotte Corday was born in 1768, at Saint-Saturnin in France. She was educated at a Roman Catholic convent in Caen, and as a young woman became a supporter of the moderate Girondins, who wanted to retain the monarchy but make reforms in France. She was in favour of the Revolution when it began in 1789, but as it progressed, like many others she became very much opposed to the destructive, violent actions of the Jacobins, such as Robespierre and his friend Marat. In 1793, the Girondins were expelled from the revolutionary convention and met at Caen to discuss how to orchestrate their opposition. Corday, who was by now a devoted party follower, was present, and heard a speech given by a leading Girondist, Jean-Pierre Brissot. In it, he denounced Marat as 'unfeeling, violent and cruel' and said that liberty could not be established again until he was dead.

Corday resolved to take matters into her own hands, and set off to Paris, determined to kill Marat herself. On 13 July 1793 she called at Marat's apartment and asked to see him, saying that she wished to 'put him in a condition to render a great service to France'. However, she was not allowed in.

That evening she returned, and was once again barred from entering Marat's room, but while she was being ejected, Marat heard the commotion and called for her to be let in.

A butcher's knife

When Corday went into Marat's chamber, she found him sitting in a large metal bath. Marat suffered from a nasty skin disease, which he claimed he had caught from hiding in the sewers of Paris. Today, the theory has been put forward that, in fact, he suffered from a severe form of herpes simplex. There was a large wooden plank over the bath, enabling him to continue writing while soaking in the tub. Legend has it that his main activity while bathing was writing out death lists.

When the female servants left the room, Corday found herself alone with Marat. She began by giving him the names of some Girondists in Caen who had spoken out against the Jacobins. Marat gleefully noted down the names of the individuals and told her that they would be rounded up the next day and sent to the guillotine. At that point, Corday whipped out a long butcher's knife hidden in her dress, and plunged it into Marat's body, severing his windpipe and piercing his lung. As the bathwater turned red, the servants reappeared, and a struggle ensued. A porter was called, who knocked her to the ground, and then tied her hands behind her back.

At her trial, Corday showed extreme bravery, making fun of the solemnity of the lawless revolutionaries and refusing to plead insanity so as to be spared. When she was sentenced to death for her crime, she said that she had nothing to say 'except that

I have succeeded'. She reiterated that she had intentionally assassinated Marat, adding, 'that is the only defence worthy of me'. On 17 July 1793, Charlotte Corday was executed. She was 25 years old.

Before she died, Corday's portrait was painted by Jean-Jacques Hauer, a National Guard officer. To thank him, she gave the artist a lock of her hair, as a souvenir 'of a poor dying woman'. At her trial, Corday had been careful to point out that she had acted alone, and said that she wished to be an example to others, especially women, in standing firm against tyranny. She called on the French to resist the brutality and violence of revolutionary demagogues such as the 'monster' Marat, and to demand a more liberal, just government. A witness to her execution, Pierre Notelet, was impressed by her courage and described her as 'calm and beautiful' at the end.

Idealized portrait

Marat's portrait was also painted to commemorate his death. David was Marat's colleague in the Convention, and was called in to arrange the funeral ceremony and to paint a realistic portrait of his friend. However, since Marat's body was now in a decomposing state, and since David himself was in a state of high emotion, the portrait turned out to be a very idealized one. Marat is portrayed in a flattering light as a healthy, young man, and when it was presented to the public, one critic claimed, 'the face expresses a supreme kindness and an exemplary revolutionary spirit carried to the point of sacrifice'. Later, when Robespierre and the Jacobins fell from grace, the painting was returned to David, but later became famous as a depiction of one of the most dramatic events of the French Revolution.

GEORGI MARKOV

In the dark annals of cold war history the story of Georgi Markov has achieved a special notoriety. Markov was a Bulgarian dissident, one of thousands of notable men and women whose political outspokenness forced them to flee the totalitarian regime of the Soviet Union, leaving friends and family behind, risking death to reach the free West. For those that remained there were show trials and the gulag, or the psychiatric hospital; for those that made it out there was usually a warm welcome from a NATO government trying to score a point in the ideological struggle between communism and capitalism. Yet, shockingly, as the fate of Georgi Markov demonstrated, escaping to the West was to prove no defence against the will of Moscow Central, whose assassins could reach with ease beyond the Iron Curtain, and leave there a stark message to all who had fled or were contemplating it: no one ever really escapes.

The target

Georgi Markov's father was a Bulgarian army officer who was classed as an enemy of the people when the Communist Party came to power in 1944. Consequently, Georgi himself was banned from attending the country's leading schools and universities. Nevertheless, by the time he was thirty-two

Bulgarian dissident Georgi Markov was killed with a poison-tipped umbrella after he had escaped to the West

According to Markov: '[Zhivkov] served the Soviet Union more ardently than the Soviet leaders themselves did.'

Nikola, living as an émigré in Bologna, Italy but instead of returning home, he stayed in Italy. He made a brief attempt to break into Italian cinema, and eventually settled in London in 1971, under the wing of the older Bulgarian dissident Peter Uvaliev, who had defected in 1947 and was now working at the BBC.

With a helping hand, perhaps, from British intelligence, Markov found work as a broadcaster in the BBC's Bulgarian section. He was also a frequent voice on Radio Free Europe and Deutsche Welle. Whenever he appeared on air he would lambast the Bulgarian government in the way that only free men could, and in quiet rooms all over Bulgaria, scores of his fellow countrymen would tune in on illicit sets. Despite heavy radio jamming on the part of the authorities it is estimated he had a regular audience of over five million.

On his desk in Sofia, the authoritarian Todor Zhivkov, Head of State from 1971 to 1989, would read the transcripts as they were handed to him by the secret police, the *Durzhavna Sigurnost* or DS. Gradually Markov roused the government's ire to the point that, when he applied for permission to return to Bulgaria and visit his dying father in 1977, he was refused. Markov's attacks on Zhivkov became more personal and frequent. Things reached a head the following year, with the emergence of the popular Bulgarian civil rights movement 'Declaration 78', which increased political pressure on Zhivkov's authoritarian government to reform. Instead, Zhivkov's minions turned their attentions towards the movement's most famous speaker, Markov.

he had become a famous literary figure and an officially approved member of the Bulgarian Writers' Union. Such was the level of his success that he was given a villa and permitted to drive a German BMW, a car practically unseen on Bulgarian roads. He certainly didn't seem like a malcontent. Nevertheless, in 1969, at forty years of age, he defected. He obtained permission from the Bulgarian government to visit his brother

Waterloo sunset

Georgi Markov's status as a target for assassination became clear in the first weeks of 1978. Radio Free Europe received a phone call from his brother Nikola in Italy, saying that he had been contacted by an anonymous member of the politburo, and told that an attack on Georgi's life was imminent. The man giving the warning claimed to be against the order, and insisted on anonymity for his own protection. Over the coming months the warnings became more frequent, and a trip to Munich was postponed because two Bulgarian agents had apparently obtained a detailed schedule of his planned movements in the German city. As time passed, however, and Markov's Munich visit passed without incident, he came round to the opinion that the Bulgarians were simply trying to scare him. KGB General Oleg Kalugin later claimed, however, that the first assassination attempt was made during this visit, but was not detected: a plan to poison the broadcaster's drink at a cocktail party.

In July, a new series of lectures, 'Markov Speaks', was broadcast by Radio Free Europe. In August he visited their headquarters in Munich for the second time that year, but admitted, for the first time, that death threats had been made directly to himself in person. In London a man had called and advised him to stop writing for the station, threatening that otherwise, he would be killed. It had happened several times, in fact, and Markov had usually hung up after making the observation that murder would only make him a martyr. The last threat had been different, however.

'Not this time,' the caller had interrupted. 'This time you will not become a martyr. You will simply die of natural causes. You will be killed by a poison that the West can neither detect nor treat.'

Markov slept poorly that night, and the next day he confided, finally, in a few trusted colleagues at the BBC. When he met his brother Nikola at Heathrow Airport a few days afterwards, Georgi apparently said, 'If they want to kill me, they can do it.' He was tired of living with the anxiety about what would happen to him.

On 7 September 1978, Markov was taking a break from a double shift at the BBC. He was walking along Waterloo Bridge when he felt a sudden stinging pain in his leg. He looked over his shoulder to see a heavy-set man bending down to pick up an umbrella, who apologized to him in a foreign accent before walking off. Markov continued to the BBC, alarmed to find that the red bump on his leg had not gone down. He became feverish, and then delirious, and died after three days of agonising pain. He left behind his wife Annabel, a BBC co-worker, and a 2 year-old daughter, Sasha.

The poison-tipped umbrella

A police autopsy found a tiny steel pellet in Markov's thigh, no more than two millimetres across. A further Ministry of Defence investigation at Porton Down, the UK's secretive military bio-chemical research base, confirmed that the pellet was hollow, and pierced in three places for the release into the bloodstream of a poison called Ricin, a substance that can be made from castor beans, and is twice as deadly as cobra venom.

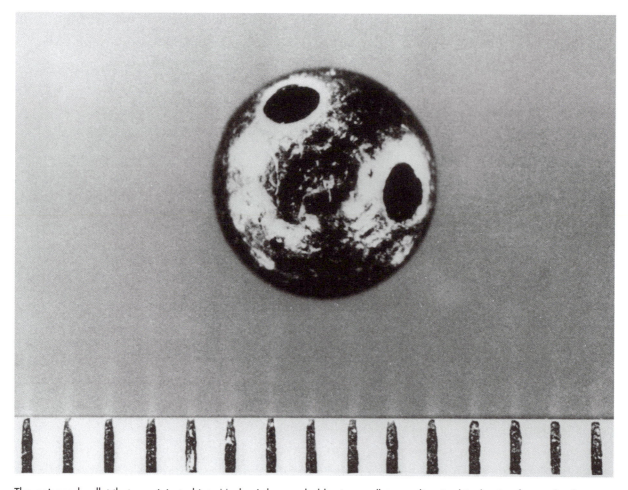

The poisoned pellet that was injected into Markov's leg, probably via a pellet gun disguised in the tip of an umbrella

Only 450 micrograms had been sufficient to kill Markov. It took months of research to verify the ricin theory, and ironically, had Markov not received a death threat, the coroner might indeed have believed he died of natural causes.

It was popularly assumed that the heavy-set stranger on Waterloo Bridge had used a poisoned umbrella to shoot or inject the ricin pellet into Markov's leg. Annabel Markov always insisted that her husband was of the opinion that the assassin had simply stooped to pick up his umbrella so he might cover his face, but the media seized on the notion of this quintessentially British symbol being turned into a weapon of death,

and the image stayed in the public mind. However, when Scotland Yard detained ex-KGB general Oleg Kalugin on his arrival at Heathrow for a BBC documentary in 1993, the old spymaster confirmed that a number of folding umbrellas had in fact been converted into poisoned pellet guns powered by compressed air for just such operations. It appears that Markov really was killed by a poison-tipped umbrella.

Farewell, Piccadilly

A shroud of mystery still hangs over the conspiracy to murder Georgi Markov, even now the Cold War has receded into history. Where did the order originate from? What parties were involved? Bulgarian and British investigators examined the case in 1989, but the relevant records were missing from Bulgarian records. In 1992, the former Bulgarian intelligence chief General Vladimir Todorov was sentenced to sixteen months in jail for destroying government files, and later the deputy interior minister committed suicide rather than go to court for the same charge. A third individual, Vasil Kostev, commonly regarded as the field officer in charge of the Markov assassination, died in an unexplained car accident.

In 1993 British police grilled a Danish man of Italian origin, Francesco Guilino, for six hours in Copenhagen. Codenamed 'Piccadilly', Guilino had allegedly worked for the DS since the 1960s, and was thought to have been the man Markov met on Waterloo Bridge. However, there was not enough evidence to bring the case to court, and Guilino was let go. Then, in 2005, a Bulgarian investigative journalist uncovered documents that confirmed Guilino as the killer. Whether he will ever be brought to justice is another matter. His DS personnel file refers to him as 'quick, cunning and fearless,' and his whereabouts have remained unknown since he sold his house in Copenhagen shortly after his interrogation.

In 2000, the Bulgarian government posthumously awarded Markov the country's highest honour, the Order of Stara Planina, for services to literature. They have yet to admit responsibility for his death. Markov is buried in Dorset, England, and his stone reads that he died in the cause of freedom.

Waterloo Brige – the scene of Markov's slow-acting assassination

CHAPTER FOUR

CELEBRITY HITS

Perhaps most disturbing of all assassinations are those of celebrities. These are the murders that are hardest to understand, often committed by people whose minds are badly disordered – who may hear voices in their heads telling them to kill, or who do so in the deluded belief that they will somehow gain approval for their actions. Often, their fascination for a star is bound up with their own feelings of inadequacy and social exclusion; they attack their victim out of a mixed set of emotions including admiration, envy, hatred and the need for attention.

Sadly, as the cult of celebrity continues to grow in our modern society, famous public figures have become the target of more and more disturbed, obsessive behaviour – whether harassment, stalking or outright hostile attack. Not surprisingly, many celebrities today surround themselves with bodyguards and make sure they have tight security controls wherever they go. However, this constrains their freedom to a large degree, and lowers their quality of life considerably. Because of these constraints, there are many famous figures who prefer to try to lead as ordinary a life as possible, moving among the public without drawing attention to themselves, in the hopes that they will be left alone to get on with their lives without any fuss. They refuse to surround themselves with bodyguards, and travel around freely, often with their families. Most of the time, this strategy works; at other times, tragically, it has proved fatal.

Such was the case of John Lennon, who by the time he died was living quietly in New York with his wife Yoko Ono and son Sean. His days as a Beatle were over; he was no longer travelling around the globe as a member of the most successful pop group on the planet, but had for many years been living in virtual retirement, in an apartment in New York's luxurious Dakota building. Ironically, when Lennon met his death in December 1980 he was experiencing something of a comeback, and had returned to recording with new optimism and enthusiasm, having overcome some of the emotional difficulties that had previously blocked his progress as an artist.

Lennon's assassin was a young man called Mark Chapman, a drifter who had developed an obsession with the star, and who apparently heard voices in his head telling him to kill his idol. In this chapter, we explore Chapman's background and the events that led up to the murder, as well as telling the story of what happened on that fateful day. In the same way, we describe the assassination of another celebrity figure, Gianni Versace, who was brutally gunned down outside his house in Miami Beach by a deranged killer who he had briefly met at a party. Also included here are the stories of other famous, powerful figures, such as the British aristocrat Lord Louis Mountbatten, the Italian anti-mafia crusader Giovanni

Falcone, the flamboyant gay Dutch politician Pim Fortuyn and – perhaps most famous of all – Archduke Franz Ferdinand, whose death triggered the First World War.

GIOVANNI FALCONE

The assassination of Judge Giovanni Falcone was a dark day in the history of the Italian nation. Falcone was known as a tireless crusader against the Mafia, a secret society whose influence had come to dominate the economy of Sicily, the largely agricultural island in the southern part of Italy. Falcone was killed in revenge for having imprisoned several major Mafia figures, and is remembered as the man courageous enough to take on the most violent, ruthless and corrupt elements in Italian society – and who lost his life as a result.

Born on 18 May 1939 in Palermo, Sicily, Giovanni Falcone grew up in a part of the city that was heavily bombed by Allied forces in 1943. His father, Arturo Falcone, was director of a chemical laboratory. Giovanni studied law at university and also attended the naval academy at Livorno, before becoming a practising lawyer. In 1964, he passed his examinations to become a judge, and after serving as a district magistrate, began to specialize in penal law.

During the 1970s, Falcone started to make a name for himself with his work on cases involving organized crime. He made many inroads in this area, including liaising with the police in the US to track down Mafia members there. He also managed to persuade several important Mafia figures, including Tomasso Buscetta, a leading member of one of the top Mafia families, to work with the police and legal authorities. Buscetta had seen many of his loved ones killed by rival families, and was among the first of the Mafia members to realize that the constant bloodshed they engaged in was entirely destructive to everyone concerned.

By the mid 1980s, Falcone was focussing on prosecuting Mafia members for a variety of crimes, including murder. Together with other magistrates, he pioneered the famous Maxi Trials, which charged and convicted hundreds of Mafia members, in an attempt to wipe out the corruption endemic in Sicilian society, thus making life safer and more prosperous for the ordinary citizen there.

For many years, the existence of a Mafia network controlling almost every aspect of the economy and bureaucracy in Sicily had been quietly ignored. There was, however, much evidence to show that this secret society had been controlling many activities since the nineteenth century, and that its influence had now penetrated into the police, legal and civil authorities. The reasons for the silence surrounding this state of affairs were twofold: first, many officials were receiving pay-offs from the Mafia and stood to gain if it continued its stranglehold on the economic life of the area; second, ordinary Sicilians were terrified of the Mafia, whose culture of machismo and violence was notorious, and whose many bloody reprisals often took place in public. For example, when Communist politician Pio La Torre suggested that Italian law

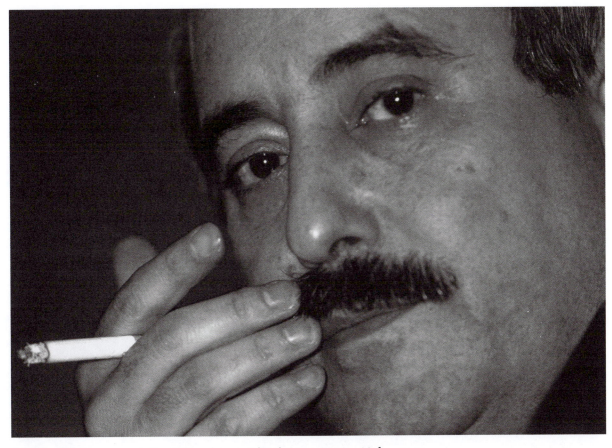

Giovanni Falcone was an Italian judge who specialized in investigating Mafia crime

should be changed to make being a member of the Mafia a criminal offence, he was shot in cold blood. The law was eventually passed, but not surprisingly, there were few other people brave enough to come forward and try to change what had become a rule of terror in Sicily.

By the 1980s, the warring families of the Mafia were engaged in tremendous conflict for control of the black economy, giving rise to hundreds of violent killings. Not only Mafiosi, but important politicians, police and legal figures were drawn into the conflict, and were murdered as well: Cesare Terranova, Rocco Chinnici, Emanuele Basile, Guiseppe Montana and Salvatore Lima, to name but a few. The victims of the 'years of lead' as the decade became known, were by

now so many that the public became outraged at this failure of the authorities to prevent complete lawlessness in the region. The politicians, many of them in the pay of the Mafia, seemed unable or unwilling to solve the problem. Something had to be done.

Enter Judge Giovanni Falcone. Together with close friend and fellow magistrate, Paolo Borsellino, Falcone led the movement to confront the situation head on. They came up with a plan to charge hundreds of Mafia members at one time, hoping that by delivering such a fatal blow, the organization would be weaker and retaliations fewer. Of course, both Falcone and Borsellino knew that they were risking their lives, but nevertheless, they continued in their work. After years of planning, they helped to bring

The aftermath of the car bomb that killed Judge Falcone and his wife

a total of four hundred and seventy-four Mafia members to trial.

On 10 February 1986, the Maxi Trial, as it was called, began in a blaze of publicity. The charges ranged from murder, drug trafficking and extortion, to being a member of the Mafia. Out of the total number of defendants, some of whom were tried in their absence, three hundred and sixty were convicted, with a total of over two thousand years in prison sentences. Some of these were important Mafia figures, such as Michele Greco, Salvatore Riina and Bernado Provenzano. There were also over a hundred acquittals, demonstrating that the exercise was not merely a 'show trial': of these, eighteen were later killed by the Mafia. One of them, Antonino Ciulla, was actually gunned down on his way to attend a celebration for his release.

Sadly, much of Falcone's work was undone by corrupt judges in the aftermath of the trial, through the appeals system. One particular judge, Corrado Carnevale, who was later found to have been taking bribes from the Mafia, became known as 'The Sentence Killer' because he let so many of the convicted men go, often on specious grounds of ill health. For example, there was one Mafia boss who claimed to be suffering from a brain tumour; he was allowed to live in a private hospital, with a crew of gangsters around him attending to his every need, despite the fact that his 'tumour' had no symptoms at all.

At the beginning of the 1990s, Falcone and Borsellino managed to recoup some of the gains made at the Maxi Trial. They managed to turn down some of the appeals, and returned several Mafiosi to prison, much to their fury. In particular, they angered Mafia boss Salvatore Riina, who had been tried in his absence, and was hoping, after his appeal, to return to his home and live in luxury for the rest of his life: instead, his appeal was turned down, and he found himself still facing a prison sentence.

On 23 May 1992, Falcone was travelling by car between the airport and the city of Palermo with his wife, Francesca Morvillo, who was also a magistrate. As the car sped along the motorway, it was blown up by a bomb placed on the side of the road. The bomb also killed three policemen. In the same year, Falcone's long-standing colleague and partner in the anti-Mafia offensive, Paolo Borsellino was also murdered in a bomb attack.

It was not long before Salvatore Riina was arrested for the crimes, which were clearly reprisal killings, in response to Falcone and Borsellino's determination to make his conviction stick. Riina was duly charged with the murder of both men, and is currently serving a life sentence for his part in the crimes. Another Mafiosi, Giovanni Brusca, was convicted of detonating the explosives that caused their deaths.

Today, the airport at Palermo has been renamed Falcone-Borsellino in honour of the two men who tried to stamp out corruption in their city and who – to some degree, at least – succeeded in doing so. According to many reports, the Mafia still holds sway in Sicily, but Falcone and Borsellino will be remembered as the men who tried to prove that the rule of law is stronger than that of brute force, and that the safety and security of ordinary citizens is of paramount importance.

LOUIS MOUNTBATTEN

Louis Mountbatten was one of the most distinguished statesmen in British history. A member of the royal family, he served as the Viceroy of India during the period of the British Empire, and after India's independence, became Governor General. He was also, like his father, head of the British Navy, as the First Sea Lord. His high-profile political career made him a target for anti-British protest, and on 27 August 1979, he was assassinated by the IRA, the Irish Republican Army, while on vacation in Donegal Bay, together with several members of his family.

His Serene Highness Louis Francis Albert Victor Nicholas Mountbatten was born on 25 June 1900 at Windsor Castle, home of the British royal family, the youngest child of Prince Louis of Battenberg. His grand-mother, Princess Alice, was the child of Britain's famous monarch Queen Victoria, and his sister (also called Alice) later became mother of Prince Philip, husband of the present British queen, Elizabeth.

Divided loyalties

When war between Britain and Germany broke out in 1914, the young boy's father Prince Louis was head of the British Royal Navy. However, since the family were so obviously of German origin, they were suspected of sympathizing with the

Lord Louis Mountbatten and Lady Mountbatten, the last Viceroy and Vicereine of India, just prior to their departure from India in 1948. He was Governor General of the Indian Union for ten months

Germans, and the Prince was forced to resign his post. Prince Louis senior also dropped his noticeably German name, Battenberg, and became Louis Mountbatten. His son Louis also gave up the fancy German names he had been born with, and was thereafter known simply as Lord Louis.

During World War One, Lord Louis made a name for himself in the British navy, and also became well known in India when he accompanied Edward, Prince of Wales, on a royal tour there. In India, he met Edwina Ashley, who later became his wife. The couple remained with each other until Edwina died, even though the marriage was a turbulent one and there were affairs on both sides. A crisis in the British monarchy occurred when Prince Edward decided to abdicate the throne in 1936; critical of Edward's behaviour, Mountbatten transferred his loyalties to the new king, his brother George.

During World War Two, Mountbatten became famous as a daring leader in the navy, and became a trusted colleague of Winston Churchill's. However, he also had

127

The state funeral of Lord Mountbatten – his draped coffin was pulled on a gun carriage and given a full military escort

his critics, who felt that some of his campaigns were misjudged, and that he – like other military leaders – was callous about the loss of life that was often involved in these manoeuvres. In particular, the failed Dieppe Raid of 1942, in which thousands of Canadian soldiers were killed, made him very unpopular in Canada. Some felt that Mountbatten's attitude helped to bring about the break-up of the British Commonwealth, especially Canada's decision to split with Britain in 1949.

Victims of carnage

Mountbatten then went on to command allied forces in South East Asia, recapturing Burma from the Japanese. After the war, Labour leader Clement Attlee appointed him Viceroy of India, and he became responsible for the transition to independence there. Despite his efforts, he was unable to prevent the partitioning of the country as India and Pakistan in 1947. Although many saw him as a peacemaker, others criticized his strategies. His wife Edwina, by contrast, was praised by everyone for her courage in helping to aid victims of the carnage that took place at the time. Towards the end of his career, Mountbatten became First Sea Lord, thus taking the post that his father had been denied many years earlier.

The Mountbatten family owned a home in Mullaghmore, County Sligo, Ireland, where they took holidays in the summer. Despite the British government's advice that the Earl and his family be given maximum security protection, Mountbatten felt it unnecessary to surround himself with policemen while he was on vacation, especially now that he was retired and out of the public eye.

In August 1979, various members of the family took a trip from Donegal Bay in their fishing yacht, the *Shadow V,* to pick up some lobster pots he had set out earlier. Unbeknown to them, a bomb had been planted in the boat by the Provisional IRA, the terrorist force who agitated for British troops to leave Ireland. As the boat sped out into the bay, the bomb went off, killing Lord Louis and three others, including the Hon. Nicholas Knatchbull, his grandson, aged fourteen, and a local boy, Paul Maxwell, aged fifteen. Others in the party were severely injured. On the same day, fifteen soldiers at a site in Warrenpoint, County Down, lost their lives in a bomb explosion.

Revenge killings

The IRA immediately issued a statement claiming responsibility for the Mountbatten attack, reporting that its members had detonated the bomb by remote control from the coast. It also took responsibility for the same-day bombing against British troops in County Down. The attacks were seen as revenge killings for Bloody Sunday, in which fourteen unarmed victims, some of them children, were shot dead by British soldiers. They had been marching through the city of Derry to protest against the internment of Catholics without trial in Northern Ireland. The incident boosted the popularity of the IRA, causing many young men to join up and engage in terrorist activities.

The Irish government strongly condemned the assassination of Lord Louis and his party, and a large memorial service took place in St Patrick's Cathedral, Dublin, to

Lord Mountbatten's body being taken away from Mullaghmore harbour, Sligo. His grandson and a local boy were also killed

commemorate his life. Local people also condemned the murder, which was thought to have been carried out by IRA members from the area around the bay, in particular the holiday town of Bundoran. On 23 November 1979, a local man, Thomas McMahon, was stopped for a routine road check. He behaved nervously, and was taken into custody, along with the driver of the vehicle, who was later acquitted. Further investigation revealed that McMahon had traces of nitroglycerine on his clothes; there was also sand and green flecks of paint on his boots, both of which were identified as coming from Mountbatten's boat at Mullaghmore. 'Bomber McMahon', as he became known to the public, was arrested, charged with the assassination, and brought to trial. He was found guilty and sentenced to life in prison.

'Bomber' McMahon

McMahon was a legendary figure in the IRA, the leader of the notorious South Armagh Brigade, a terrorist organization that had been responsible for the deaths of over a hundred British soldiers. The IRA had sent McMahon to Libya to study terrorist tactics, including the use of detonators and explosives. Although experts believed the Mountbatten attack to be the work of a group, McMahon was the only person to be convicted of the crime. He was released in 1998 as part of a peace deal for Northern Ireland, which caused a good deal of controversy. Since his release, McMahon has claimed that he no longer has links with the IRA and is training to be a carpenter – a fitting trade, perhaps, for a man who

reduced the yacht of Lord Louis Mountbatten to matchsticks, on that fateful summer day in August 1979.

GIANNI VERSACE

The murder of Gianni Versace horrified the media when it took place on 15 July 1997. At the time, Versace was at the height of his success as one of the foremost fashion designers in the world, having designed highly glamorous, flamboyant clothes for rock stars such as Elton John. With his trademark T-shirts and unstructured suits, designed for the TV series *Miami Vice*, Versace had also pioneered a relaxed look for men that had become synonymous with 1980s style. His killer was Andrew Cunanan, a gay man who inhabited the fringes of Versace's social world, and whose apparent frustrations with his lack of success erupted in a killing spree that was as violent as it was senseless. After killing a string of men, both friends and strangers, Cunanan travelled to Miami and lay in wait for Versace, shooting him on the front steps of his palatial home, Casa Casuarina, at South Beach. Afterwards, the killer fled and went into hiding. He was found eight days later on a houseboat, having committed suicide.

Gianni Versace was born on 2 December 1946 in Calabria, Italy. His father sold electrical goods and his mother owned a dressmaking store. As a boy, Gianni learned the tailoring trade, both sewing and designing clothes. In 1972, he began receiving commissions to design for clothing companies and later opened his own store.

Gianni Versace at the height of his career in 1994

A couple look on in shock at the blood-stained steps of Versace's Miami Beach villa on Ocean Drive

During the 1980s, his own collections became hugely popular, and he became known as the designer who dispensed with the old-fashioned tie, yet still managed to make his men look stylish and well-groomed. He also began to dress some of the most famous names of the day, in the world of film, pop and even royalty – Princess Diana was one of his close friends. By the 1990s, along with Ralph Lauren and Giorgio Armani, he had become one of only a handful of world-famous designers with a huge clothing empire to his name.

Glamorous lifestyle

By the time he reached fifty, Versace had about as much success as any man could want, and was talking about leading a more relaxed life with more time for entertaining. He had bought a large property on Ocean Drive, overlooking the sea at Miami Beach, and transformed it into an Italianate palace for himself and his friends. At the time, Miami Beach was the hub of a fashionable gay social life, and there was an array of ever-changing restaurants and clubs to see and be seen in. However, there was also a darker side to this sophisticated world of money, glamour and power; AIDS was terrifying the gay community, and there was a constant undertow of drug abuse and violent sex lurking below the glittering surface of the Californian gay lifestyle.

Enter Andrew Cunanan, a good-looking, personable young man who became part of this lifestyle but who – unlike Gianni Versace – never had the talent or application to do more than drift on its treacherous currents. Cunanan was born on 31 August 1969. His father, Modesto, was Filipino, a fact that Andrew later often disguised, pretending that he came from a Latino background instead. His mother, Mary Ann, was a strict Catholic, and was not happy with her husband, who was something of an authoritarian. Modesto's job in the hospital corps of the navy often took him away from home, and when he returned he often became paranoid that his wife had been having affairs, even accusing her of giving birth to a child that was not his.

The couple had four children, the youngest of whom was Andrew. When Andrew was born, his mother suffered a bout of depression, and he was mainly cared for by his father. Andrew grew up to be extremely bright with a high IQ but often played the fool, finding it difficult to settle down to work at school. The tensions of his home life were evident in his behaviour, but people found him entertaining and fun, and on the whole accepted his obvious homosexuality from a young age.

Selling sex

From the age of about fifteen, Andrew began to frequent gay bars and clubs, often changing his name and appearance and making up stories about his life. Before long, he was selling his body as a male prostitute to rich, older men and spending the money on flashy new designer clothes. His parents had no idea what was going on, but they were having troubles of their own. Modesto had changed his employment and become a stockbroker, but had lost money and the couple split up. Modesto returned to the Philippines. Andrew quarrelled with his

Frustrated with his life, Andrew Cunanan (left) went on a killing spree which included gunning down Gianni Versace

mother and followed his father there, but was horrified to find him living in squalor, and soon returned – after prostituting himself once again to earn the fare home.

New life

Once back in America, Andrew carved out a new life for himself in San Francisco, often posing as a young naval officer. There, he began to lead the high life, and once actually met and chatted briefly to Gianni Versace at a party. At the same time, his life was beginning to spin out of control. He was acting in gay porn videos, some of them very violent, and his self-destructive mood was beginning to sour. He was drinking excessively, and became angry and unpredictable with friends; he was paranoid that he had AIDS, but was afraid to seek medical help; and he was also broke, having been abandoned by his rich lovers. For reasons that are still unclear, Cunanan's anger suddenly spilled over into violence, and he accused two ex-boyfriends, Jeff Trail and David Madson, of having an affair with each other. The men were both well-to-do, which also fuelled Cunanan's jealousy. Cunanan's behaviour became abusive and he telephoned Trail, threatening to kill him. He then went to visit Madson in Minneapolis, who tried to reassure him by inviting Trail over to his house, but a bitter argument broke out. Cunanan found a hammer in the kitchen and clubbed Trail over the head with it repeatedly, smashing his skull and killing him. Madson panicked, and helped Cunanan roll the body up in a rug; and a couple of days later, the pair took off together in Madson's jeep. Later, Cunanan inexplicably pulled a gun on Madson and shot him, killing him as well.

The next two victims were complete strangers. The first was an elderly man named Lee Miglin who was standing outside his house when Cunanan approached for directions. He took Miglin into the garage, bound, tortured and killed him before spending the night in the house and taking off in Miglin's car the next day. The second was 45-year-old William Reese, the caretaker of a cemetery, whom he held up and shot.

Shot twice in the head

Amazingly, Cunanan managed to escape the police, who were by now on his trail, and hole up in Miami Beach. There, he checked into a hotel, dined in restaurants and wandered the streets for two months without anybody noticing him – a fact that caused much criticism of the local police force when it came to light after Versace's killing. During this time, he followed Versace's movements, and noted that the designer often went to a café on his own in the mornings. On the morning of 15 July 1997, he followed Versace home from the café and shot him twice in the head as he was opening the gate of his house.

The fact that Versace was so famous prompted the FBI to launch a huge search for the killer, who was found eight days later, hiding out on a private houseboat. A caretaker discovered Cunanan there and alerted the police, who surrounded the houseboat. A dramatic standoff took place, with Cunanan refusing to come out and give himself up. When the police finally moved in, they found Cunanan dead on the floor. He had shot himself with his murdered friend Jeff Trail's pistol.

Post-mortem

A post-mortem revealed that Cunanan was not suffering from AIDS, despite the rumours that this was what had sent him over the edge and caused his demonic behaviour. It still remains unclear exactly what motivated Cunanan, beyond a generalized sense of jealousy and anger at the world. Because of this, since Versace's death, there have been conspiracy theories to explain what happened, including the theory that his assassination was master-minded by the Mafia. However, it seems that, to date, no one has a clear answer as to exactly why Versace met his death that day, and the murder will continue to puzzle commentators for many years to come.

JOHN LENNON

The assassination of John Lennon on 8 December 1980 shocked his many fans worldwide, and turned the former Beatle into an icon – or even a saint – almost overnight. Despite the fact that, by the time he was murdered, the reclusive star had undergone long periods of creative inactivity, and was reported at various times to have been violent, drug-addicted, alcoholic and mentally unbalanced, after his death his reputation grew until he became, not only one of the seminal figures of popular music during the twentieth century, but a figurehead for peace and love, attracting a loyal following among rising generations of new fans – which he continues to do to this day.

'Bigger than Jesus'

Born in Liverpool on 9 October 1940, John Lennon was the son of a merchant seaman and grew up in a working-class area of Liverpool, England. His parents, Julia and Alf, split up when he was five, his father abandoning the family. Julia was left to cope on her own, and found herself unable to, so John was sent to live with his aunt Mimi. He continued to see his mother Julia, with whom he had a troubled relationship. She taught him to play the banjo, which gave him a distinctive style when he later picked up the guitar.

When Lennon was seventeen, Julia was killed in a car accident and he was obliged to go to the morgue to identify her body, an incident which scarred him emotionally for

The iconic image of John Lennon and his wife, Yoko Ono, during their famous 'make love not war' protest in 1969

David Chapman being interviewed by Barbara Walters on the US TV show *20/20* in 1980

life. As a young man, Lennon went to art school but dropped out, instead forming a band called *The Silver Beetles* with Paul McCartney and George Harrison. In 1962, Lennon married his girlfriend Cynthia Powell and became the father of a son, Julian.

The band, whose name was soon shortened to 'The Beatles' went on to tour Germany, and eventually achieved worldwide success. Crucial to their popularity were the songs of Lennon and McCartney, which developed from the bright, melodic pop of the early sixties to the introspective psychedelia of their later

period. The Beatles became one of the most influential bands of their time, not only musically but in terms of the new 1960s counterculture in general, and their opinions were asked on every question under the sun. Lennon took the opportunities offered to him by his fame to express his often controversial beliefs, sometimes adding ironic comments that people took seriously, such as that The Beatles were 'more popular than Jesus'. This particular remark infuriated the Christian church, and Lennon was roundly condemned by many members of the establishment.

Lennon's personal life also became the

subject of controversy after he divorced his wife Cynthia and married artist Yoko Ono. Together, the pair recorded experimental albums and conducted a series of attention-grabbing public protests, including lying in bed surrounded by posters for peace and receiving members of the press for interviews. Because of stunts such as these, certain sections of the media presented Lennon and Yoko as laughably eccentric, but in retrospect, there is no doubt that they drew attention to several important political causes at the time, such as the war in Vietnam.

Acrimonious disputes

As well as the establishment and the media, there were many fans of the Beatles who felt that Ono's influence on Lennon was a negative one. Lennon began to include his wife in every aspect of the band's recording work, and she became a constant presence everywhere he went. Ono's influence, and other issues to do with leadership of the group, eventually caused Lennon's relationship with The Beatles to break down. There followed a series of acrimonious disputes with Paul McCartney and the other Beatles, after which Lennon recorded as a solo artist and with Ono, until his retirement in 1975 following the birth of his second son, Sean. In 1980, Lennon returned to the studio, recording an album, *Double Fantasy*. At this time, shortly before his murder, he appeared to have come out of a fallow creative period in his life, to the delight of his fans.

During the 1960s, Lennon had once been asked how he thought he would die, and had replied that he expected to be 'popped off by some loony'. He had also expressed anxiety, in later years, that he was being stalked. (In part this was based on a well-founded belief that the FBI were harassing him, in order to bar him from living in the US because of his political activities; and there were, of course, numerous fans who followed him everywhere, making security a constant issue for him and his entourage.) As it turned out, these words, delivered in his humorous, offhand way, eventually proved prophetic.

The killer

On Saturday 6 December 1980, a young man named Mark Chapman checked into the YMCA on 63rd Street, just off Central Park West in New York City. A drifter, Chapman had been born in Texas on 10 May 1955. He had grown up in Georgia, an overweight child who was unpopular at school. In his teens he became a committed Christian and youth worker. In despair after a failed relationship, he moved to Hawaii where he planned to kill himself. When his suicide attempt failed, he found a renewed appetite for life. He met and married his Japanese American wife, Gloria, and things went well for a couple of years. Gradually, however, his behaviour became increasingly eccentric and he developed an obsession with John Lennon. Strangely, he was also obsessed with the J. D. Salinger novel, *The Catcher in the Rye*. When Chapman heard that John Lennon had a new record out he felt compelled to meet his idol.

That Saturday, Chapman spent several hours outside the Dakota building, clutching a copy of *Double Fantasy*, waiting for

Lennon to appear. When he did not, Chapman retreated to the YMCA for the night. Next day, he moved to the nearby Sheraton Hotel and returned to his vigil. Once again Lennon failed to show, and Chapman contented himself with buying a copy of *Playboy* featuring a John Lennon interview. That night he called an escort agency, but when the call girl arrived told her he merely wanted to talk to her, just as Holden Caulfield, the hero of *The Catcher In The Rye*, had done in a similar situation. He paid her $190 when she left at 3 a.m.

Next morning at 10.30 a.m. he woke up, took out the hotel Bible, opened it to the beginning of the St. John Gospel, and wrote in the word 'Lennon' after 'John'. Then he picked up his copy of *Double Fantasy* and his gun, and headed off to the Dakota building, picking up a copy of *The Catcher In The Rye* from a bookstore on the way.

Autograph

Once at the Dakota building he became so engrossed in the book that he didn't notice Lennon entering the building. He continued to wait and chatted with other Lennon fans. Soon after lunchtime a fellow fan spotted five-year-old Sean Lennon coming out with his nanny. Chapman shook the child's hand. During the course of the afternoon he saw other celebrities including Lauren Bacall and Paul Simon coming and going. Finally, around six o'clock, John Lennon came out with Yoko Ono, heading for a recording studio. Chapman offered him the record to sign and Lennon did so graciously, asking him, 'Is that all you want?'

Part of him, Chapman said later, was satisfied with this, wanted to take his autograph and go home to Hawaii and get on with his life. Another part of him, however, had a much darker purpose in mind, and that part won out.

Chapman continued to wait outside the Dakota building. At around 10.50 p.m. John and Yoko returned from the recording studio. Yoko Ono got out of the white limousine first.

This is what happened next, by Chapman's own account, as given to the police a few hours later: 'He walked past me, and then a voice in my head said, "Do it, do it, do it," over and over again, saying "Do it, do it, do it, do it," like that. I pulled the gun out of my pocket. I handed it over to my left hand. I don't remember aiming. I must have done it, but I don't remember drawing the bead or whatever you call it. And I just pulled the trigger steady five times.'

Lennon tried to get away from the gun, but four of the five bullets hit him. Even so he managed to run up six steps into the concierge's station. There he said the words, 'I'm shot', then fell face down.

Dead on arrival

Chapman, meanwhile, just stayed where he was. He got out his copy of *The Catcher in The Rye* and started reading, waiting for the police to arrive. Then he put his hands in the air and surrendered, saying 'I acted alone.' Lennon was rushed in a police car to St Luke's Roosevelt Hospital, but died soon after his arrival. Within hours there was a crowd of thousands of people outside the hospital. The following day the whole world seemed to be united in mourning of a kind

Pim Fortuyn was a popular politician in his native Netherlands, tipped by some to become the next prime minister

not seen since the Kennedy assassination.

Mark Chapman was arrested, brought to trial, and pleaded guilty to murder. He was convicted and sentenced to a term of life imprisonment. He is still serving his sentence, despite several parole hearings, at least in part because the authorities firmly believe it to be highly likely that Chapman would be himself murdered were he ever to be released.

PIM FORTUYN

The assassination of Pim Fortuyn, a charismatic, openly gay Dutch politician who was tipped in some quarters to become prime minister, caused a national outcry in Europe when it occurred on 6 May 2002. He was shot in cold blood by a white Dutchman, Volkert van der Graaf, who said he had committed the crime in an effort to protect social minorities in the country, but seemed to have a vague political agenda. Fortuyn had become a controversial figure as a result of speaking out against Muslim leaders in the Netherlands, warning that they threatened the country's well-known tradition of liberalism, especially in respect of gay rights. He had also called for an end to all immigration into the Netherlands, especially by Muslims. By the end of his life he had become a very popular politician, who threatened to topple the consensus of Dutch politics with his controversial policies, which mixed left- and right-wing ideas. His brutal murder was the first political killing in the Netherlands for four hundred years, and shocked the Dutch public, where politicians were used to travelling around without tight security.

Flamboyant figure

Wilhelmus Simon Petrus Fortuijn, nicknamed Pim, was born on 19 February 1948 in the town of Velsen, Holland. He grew up in a Catholic family, and went on to study at university in Amsterdam. He later became a lecturer in sociology, first at the Nijenrode Institute, and then at Groningen University, where he became a professor. He then made a career change into government administration and moved to Rotterdam. After that, he became a professor at Erasmus University before changing career once again, this time to become a newspaper columnist and public speaker. He also wrote a number of books. He became widely known in Holland as a flamboyant figure who lived alone in a beautiful house with his

two King Charles spaniels, often travelling with them by limousine. He loved expensive clothes, and did nothing to disguise his evident homosexuality. As his fame grew, he became more and more involved in politics, and was never afraid to voice his controversial views.

In November 2001, he became part of the Leefbaar Nederland party (translated as 'the Livable Netherlands party'). He soon won local elections in the Rotterdam district, ousting the Labour party there, which had been in power for decades. His popularity ensured that he became a top candidate for the national elections in the following year. As a result, he was interviewed as to his political manifesto by a Dutch newspaper, the *Volkskrant*. In the interview, he announced that he wished to curb immigration of people from Islamic countries, an opinion that caused his immediate ejection from the Leefbaar party. In response, Fortuyn set up his own party, the Lijst Pim Fortuyn, attracting many followers from the Leefbaar to his cause.

Opinions in the Netherlands were divided as to Fortuyn's political aims. Some felt that he was voicing the feelings of the vast majority of Dutch people, who were frightened by some of the teachings of fundamentalist Islamic leaders. For example, there had been speeches in some Mosques about Westerners being 'lower than pigs' for tolerating homosexuality, while other teachers had exhorted their listeners to beat their wives in order to discipline them. Fortuyn stated that this was against the spirit of Western democracy, and that the existence of separate Muslim communities in which these views were expressed was a threat to the democratic Dutch tradition of tolerance, and an attack on the values of liberalism and equal rights in the country. On the other hand, others pointed out that Fortuyn's anti-Muslim stance caused a great deal of trouble for Muslim communities, who found themselves being seen as scapegoats. Some commentators felt that his views were racist, and that his approach would lead to the persecution of Muslims, in the same way that the Jews had been persecuted in the Second World War.

Shot in the back and head

Not surprisingly, Fortuyn became the centre of a political controversy in Holland, but one that was conducted democratically, without violence, in the usual way. However, this was not to last. On 6 May 2002, nine days before the national election, he went to a radio station in the town of Hilversum, gave an interview, and then walked through the parking lot to his car. On the way, he was shot several times at short range, and bled to death. The assassin fled the scene. The driver of Fortuyn's car, Hans Smolders, chased the attacker, who was arrested shortly afterwards, still holding the gun he had used. He was arrested, charged with the murder and brought to trial.

Later, the details of what happened on that fateful day emerged. Van der Graaf had apparently used the Internet to find out exactly where Fortuyn was scheduled to appear, and had printed out a map of the radio station. He had bought a pistol and cartridges, illegally, and had loaded seven of the cartridges into his gun. On the day of the

assassination, he had gone to work in the normal way, carrying the gun in his rucksack. He had told colleagues he was taking the afternoon off, and had driven to Hilversum. When he reached the town, he had parked his car and walked to the radio station, where he hid in some bushes until Fortuyn came out. When he saw his victim appear, he had walked towards him and had begun to shoot, firing a total of six shots at him. Five of them had hit Fortuyn in the back and head, whereupon Van der Graaf had run away, pursued by Fortuyn's driver, Hans Smolders.

As Smolders ran after Van der Graaf, two office workers joined in the chase. Van der Graaf had his gun in his jacket pocket, and occasionally held it up to put them off. However, they continued to chase him, until eventually they reached a main road, where Van der Graaf took out his pistol and pointed it at Smolders. Smolders had been reporting what was going on to police, using his cell phone, while he was running along behind Van der Graaf. The police were waiting for Van der Graaf at a petrol station down the road, where they met him with guns raised, so that the assassin immediately gave himself up.

Cold-blooded murder

The question on everyone's minds, by the time the case came to court, was whether Van der Graaf was insane, or whether he had planned the murder and assassinated Fortuyn in cold blood. There was also the question of whether he had acted alone, or as part of a conspiracy. As it transpired, Van der Graaf was an environmental activist, with a particular interest in animal rights (something that Fortuyn had seldom commented on). He had set up and run an organization that looked into violations of animal rights, in intensive farming and the fur trade. He had a girlfriend and a young child, and was described as an emotionally withdrawn individual, who seemed to be under stress after the birth of his child. - Before the trial, Van der Graaf was assessed by expert psychiatrists, who diagnosed him as suffering from an obsessive-compulsive disorder; however, they added that this would not have caused him to commit murder, and thus declared him sane. The idea that he acted as part of a terrorist group was also ruled out.

Van der Graaf was convicted, and sentenced to eighteen years' imprisonment, much to the disappointment of Fortuyn's supporters, who felt he should have received a life sentence. The defendant was impassive and expressionless as the verdict was read out.

THEO VAN GOGH

Theo van Gogh, a descendant of the famous painter Vincent van Gogh, was a friend and admirer of Pim Fortuyn's. A controversial newspaper columnist, film maker, and actor, Theo van Gogh was known for writing vitriolic attacks on public figures, especially politicians. These were often extremely offensive and caused him to be sacked from various media jobs, as well as involving him in several lawsuits. Fortuyn was one of the few to escape Van Gogh's poison pen; Van Gogh liked Fortuyn's outspokenness, and the way he liked to shock the 'politically correct' establishment in the Netherlands; he often referred to the shaven-headed Pym as 'the divine baldhead'. Van Gogh himself was something of a notorious figure in Dutch society: he chain-smoked, used drugs such as cocaine, drank heavily, and had a generally pessimistic outlook on life. He liked to bait minority groups, and made offensive remarks about the Jewish Holocaust, which understandably angered the Jewish community. He was particularly vociferous in his criticism of the Muslim religion; like Fortuyn, he complained that the forces of Islam were threatening to undermine the traditional, liberal values of the Netherlands. Much of his polemic was simply vulgar abuse, but it served to inflame an already tense situation, especially in urban areas where Muslim communities were rapidly growing.

Throat slit

After the assassination of Pim Fortuyn, Van Gogh found another favourite in Ayaan Hirsi Ali, the Somali-born Dutch politician who had spoken out against the treatment of women in some parts of Africa. Working with Van Gogh, Ali wrote a script for a ten-minute film, *Submission*, which concerned the abuse of Muslim women – a subject close to her heart. The film showed the women with apparently anti-feminist verses from the Koran painted on to their semi-naked bodies. The film caused a stir on its release in 2004, and both the film maker and script writer were subjected to death threats. Van Gogh was advised to take security measures, but refused – a decision that cost him

The outspoken Van Gogh refused to give in before the tyranny of fundamentalist regimes – a fact that cost him his life

The body of Theo van Gogh lies on an Amsterdam street, killed on his way to work. His murderer was arrested at the scene

his life.

On 2 November 2004, in the early morning, Van Gogh was murdered as he walked along the street. A Muslim assassin, 26-year-old Mohammed Bouyeri, shot him, firing eight bullets into his body. The assassin then stabbed his victim, leaving two knives plunged into his chest. He also slit Van Gogh's throat. A note pinned to one of the knives threatened revenge on Ali, who immediately went into hiding. To date, she remains under heavy security.

Bouyeri was arrested and brought to trial, where it emerged that he was part of a suspected Dutch terrorist organization, the Hofstad Network. To many people's surprise,

he was not a recent immigrant, but had been born in the Netherlands, of Moroccan parentage. After the death of his mother, his father had remarried, and he had turned to the fundamentalist Islamic faith, wearing a djellaba, growing a beard and visiting the mosque frequently, where he was thought to have made contact with radical Muslims. After his arrest for the murder of Van Gogh, Bouyeri continued to uphold his anti-western position as an anti-western Muslim, claiming that he had killed Van Gogh as part of his duty to Islam. Because of his strong anti-democratic stance, his crime was taken extremely seriously by the Dutch authorities. He was convicted of the murder, as well as

Amsterdam-born Mohammed Bouyeri killed Van Gogh because of the film Van Gogh made which condemned Islam

Archduke Ferdinand (left) was a high-ranking member of the Hapsburg dynasty and the future heir to the Austro-Hungarian throne

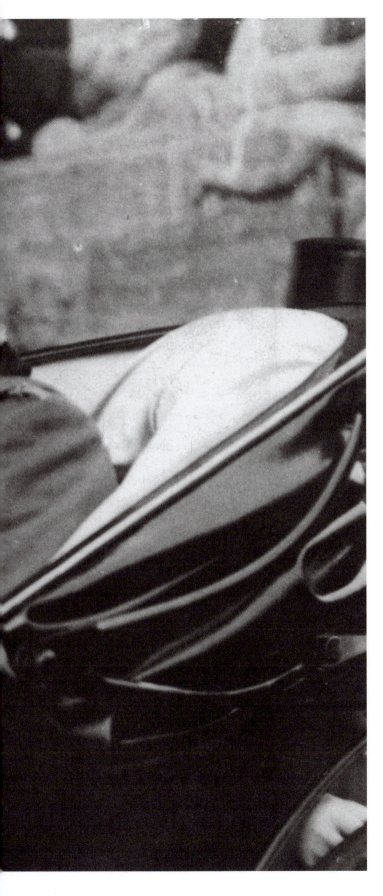

other charges, and was sentenced to a term of life imprisonment.

ARCHDUKE FERDINAND

The assassination of Archduke Franz Ferdinand at Sarajevo, Bosnia-Herzegovina, on 28 June 1914 is perhaps the most well-known assassination of all time. For many years, schoolchildren were taught that the killing of the heir to the Austro-Hungarian throne was the event that plunged Europe into the First World War, which went on to become one of the most horrific and destructive wars of the twentieth century. However, today the assassination is seen in a rather different light, as the event that sparked off the war, rather than the event that actually caused it.

Trail of devastation

It is certainly true to say that, as a result of the assassination, Austria declared war on Serbia, and the Balkan states became embroiled in a massive conflict that eventually drew in Germany and Britain. However, in retrospect it is clear that the problem was, from the start, a conflict between these two major European powers for economic and political control of the rest of the world. Since Victorian times, Britain had built up a huge, powerful empire; and subsequently, from the turn of the century, Germany began to challenge that power, seeking to expand its trade and military might in the same way that Britain had done. Given this situation, it seemed that conflict between the two superpowers was bound to erupt at some point; and many historians believe that, even if the archduke had not been assassinated on that fateful day, war would still have broken out sooner or later.

Be that as it may, the assassination of Franz Ferdinand still holds a place as one of the most significant and memorable events in history, sparking off, as it did, the outbreak of World War One. For this reason, there are many detailed accounts of the assassination, though there still remain some questions that have never been answered.

Cheering crowds

Archduke Franz Ferdinand was an extremely high-ranking member of the Hapsburg dynasty. The nephew of Emperor Franz Josef I of Austria, he was the future heir to the Austro-Hungarian throne. His politics were relatively liberal, considering he was a member of one of the oldest and wealthiest dynastic houses of Europe. Ferdinand was in favour of keeping the peace between the warring nations of the Balkans, and also supported liberal causes such as giving the vote to all citizens of all classes (as long as they were male, that is). These views, of course, did not endear him to the higher echelons of the aristocracy in Austria, who were terrified that his plans would end their privileged way of life. It was even suspected, after the assassination, that the killing was a plot by the Austro-Hungarian establishment to rid themselves of the archduke, who was seen as a threat to their privilege and power. However, no evidence has ever been uncovered to

support such a theory, and it remains in the realms of conjecture.

On the day in question, 28 June 1914, Archduke Franz Ferdinand and his wife, Countess Sophie, paid a formal visit to General Oskar Potiorek, the governor of the Austrian provinces of Bosnia-Herzegovina, who had invited them to watch a parade of his troops. Although Ferdinand knew that the visit would be dangerous, and that there was a threat of terrorist attack from Bosnian Serb nationalists, who wanted freedom and independence from the Austrian empire, he accepted the invitation.

In order to escape attention from the terrorists, the archduke and Countess Sophie arrived unannounced by train. However, they then made the mistake of riding through the streets with their host, Oskar Potiorek, in an open-roofed car. Crowds of people turned out to greet them, and they waved happily back, obviously relying on their security forces to deal with any potential troublemakers among the cheering populace.

Suicide bombers

All went well until, just after ten o'clock, the cortège of cars passed the police station of the city, where a young man called Nedeljko Cabrinovic was waiting. Cabrinovic was a member of a terrorist organization known as the Black Hand. Their leader Dragutin Dimitrijevic had managed to persuade its young members to assassinate the archduke, even to die in the course of their duties if necessary. To this end, Dimitrijevic had handed out vials of cyanide to the men, in case they were arrested. Thus, armed with

Archduke Ferdinand and his pregnant wife, Countess Sophie, just one hour before they were assassinated

guns and bombs, the assassins set out, taking up different positions in the crowd so as to make sure that, one way or another, their target would be hit.

Failed first attempt

Among the jostling crowds, it did not prove easy for the terrorists to pull out their guns, get the archduke in their sights, take aim, and fire. The first terrorist to make an attempt failed altogether, missing the cavalcade of cars as it passed along the streets. The next attempt was slightly more successful. Cabrinovic, who had been

hiding in a small back street, moved forward and threw a bomb at the archduke's car, which ended up hitting the car behind. Panic broke out as some of the passengers in the car were injured. A few members of the crowd were also hurt.

Terrified of being captured, Cabrinovic immediately swallowed his vial of cyanide, and rushed down to the river to jump in and drown himself. However, the river turned out to be rather shallow and as he stood in a few feet of water, he was arrested by the police.

Although he had taken the cyanide,

The arrest photo of Gavrilo Princip (second from the right). He succeeded where two others that day had failed

Cabrinovic survived, as he was unable to control the spasms that caused him to vomit it up. He was brought to trial, convicted and received a fifteen-year prison sentence. Conditions in prison proved extremely harsh, especially after the outbreak of the First World War, and he went on to die at a young age of tuberculosis.

A fateful decision

Despite the fact that Cabrinovic had failed to hit his target, his action brought the archduke and Countess Sophie closer to danger. On the way to visit the troops, the Archduke decided that he would pay a visit to one of the injured citizens at the local hospital and, accordingly, asked his driver to take a different route. The driver followed instructions, but unfortunately lost his way in the process, and ended up driving down Franz Josef Street, one of the small back streets of the city.

Purely by chance, one of the other terrorists from the Black Hand group, a young man named Gavrilo Princip, was eating a sandwich in the Moritz Schiller café on this street. He had obviously thought the opportunity to kill the archduke was now over, and was unwinding over a meal after the event.

Princip was a 19-year-old who was dedicated to ridding Bosnia of the Austrian imperialists. As well as being a member of Black Hand, he also belonged to a group of political activists called Young Bosnia. Along with his comrades, he had turned out that day to try to shoot the archduke, but had been unable to get near the car because of the large crowds. Now, as the car passed by the window of the café, he suddenly leapt into action, seizing the opportunity to run out into the street and re-attempt the mission he and his friends had set for themselves that morning.

By this time, the driver of the car, realizing he was lost, was backing slowly down the street. Away from the crowds, it was an easy enough task for Princip to take out his revolver, aim carefully and shoot at the passengers, who were now only a few feet away from him.

Fatal shootings

The first passenger to be shot was Countess Sophie, who was hit in the stomach. Sadly, she was pregnant at the time. She collapsed in front of her horrified husband, and died within minutes. The archduke could hardly believe what was happening, and seemed to think at first his wife had just fainted. He tried to rouse her, but was then shot in the neck himself. After a few minutes, he also died.

Like his comrade Cabrinovic, Gavrilo Princip had taken a vial of cyanide before the police came to arrest him. And, again like Cabrinovic, the cyanide failed to kill him. After his arrest, he was brought to trial, convicted and received a twenty-year prison sentence. Had he been older, he would have received a death sentence. As it was, in the same way as his comrade, he died of tuberculosis only a few years later, while still in prison.

A turning point in history?

Many commentators today have speculated on what would have happened if the car driving the archduke had not made the fatal error of turning into the wrong street, giving Princip the opportunity to kill the heir to the Austrian throne. Could World War One perhaps have been averted if the assassination had not taken place, and all the attempts had failed?

Like most 'what if' questions in history, the answer is not clear; but with the benefit of hindsight, we can see that tension was mounting in Europe, and that sooner or later, war was likely to break out. Whether or not the conflict would have escalated so quickly, and resulted in a war of such epic proportions, especially in regard to the numbers who lost their lives, remains a matter of conjecture.

CHAPTER FIVE

NEAR MISSES

The assassinations we have explored so far have gone down in history as significant, important events. Some of them, such as the assassinations of Archduke Franz Ferdinand, US Presidents Abraham Lincoln and John F. Kennedy, Indian premier Mahatma Gandhi, and US civil rights leader Martin Luther King, may even have changed the course of world history. But almost as fascinating, if not more so, are those assassination attempts that failed.

The famous figures we deal with here have all, with the exception of artist Andy Warhol, lived under the threat of assassination for most of their public lives. For King Hussein of Jordan, the threat of assassination hung over him since childhood. He was only a young boy when, in 1951, he accompanied his grandfather King Abdullah I to prayers in Jerusalem. As they were climbing the steps to the mosque, a gunman shot his grandfather, who lay bleeding on the ground beside him until he died. Hussein was shot at too, and narrowly escaped death. After the abdication of his father Talal, who was mentally imbalanced, Hussein succeeded the throne. During his turbulent reign, as he tried to maintain a balance between warring Palestinian and Israeli forces, at the same time maintaining close ties with the West, he was subject to constant assassination attempts, culminating in a terrifying shooting on the outskirts of Amman. Gunmen opened fire on his car, injuring

the driver. However, miraculously once again, Hussein survived the attack.

In the same way, major figures throughout history were subject to repeated assassination attempts – and survived. Queen Elizabeth I of England, known as 'Good Queen Bess', spent much of her reign in fear of her life, as hostility between Catholic and Protestants elements within the country mounted. Mary, Queen of Scots, the leader of the Catholic contingent, was suspected of constantly plotting to kill Queen Elizabeth, so Elizabeth had her imprisoned for many years. In the end, when Mary continued to conspire against her, Elizabeth was forced to put her to death. Elizabeth herself lived to a ripe old age, having managed to avoid assassination during her long and celebrated reign.

In modern times, there are several contemporary figures who have managed an equally difficult task, including Fidel Castro, President of Cuba. For many years, the CIA and American security forces plotted to assassinate him, coming up with ideas worthy of a James Bond movie script – which included exploding cigars, a diving suit impregnated with a lethal fungus, and other extraordinary devices. All these plans failed, and to this day, Castro continues to rule Cuba, despite America's constant attempts over the years to topple him – ranging from all-out invasion of the country to secret murder conspiracies.

In this chapter, we take a look at some of

these indomitable figures, from Castro to French President Charles de Gaulle, from Nazi demagogue Adolf Hitler to Catholic pontiff Pope John Paul, and from British premier Margaret Thatcher to pop art socialite Andy Warhol, showing how a combination of courage and cunning helped them to outwit their assassins and live to tell their stories.

ELIZABETH I

The reign of Elizabeth I is one of the most celebrated periods in English history. From 1558 until 1603, 'the Virgin Queen', as she became known, ruled over the country, surviving tremendous religious and political turmoil, which included a number of assassination attempts.

The most notorious of these was by Mary, Queen of Scots, whose plotting to gain the English throne was a constant thorn in Elizabeth's side. Eventually, after imprisoning Mary for many years, Elizabeth's counsellors and ministers pressured her into putting her rival to death for treason, and the Scottish queen was executed by royal decree. However, after Mary's death, Elizabeth was wracked with guilt, especially at having executed a fellow queen, and went on to become extremely paranoid about plots and assassination attempts against her. Given the turmoil of the times, and the repeated attempts on her life, it was something of a miracle that Elizabeth eventually died of natural causes, as an old lady, still unmarried, on 24 March 1603.

'Bloody Mary'

Elizabeth was born on 7 September 1533, the daughter of King Henry VIII and Ann Boleyn, whom he had married in secret. Furious with Ann Boleyn for not having produced a son, he had his wife beheaded on charges of treason, witchcraft and incest with her elder brother. After her mother's death, Elizabeth was stripped of her title as princess and declared to be illegitimate. King Henry went on to marry a succession of wives, and when he died, his son Edward became the next king. However, Edward VI died young, and the next to succeed the throne was the Catholic daughter of Catherine of Aragon, Mary Tudor, also known as 'Bloody Mary' because of her habit of torturing Protestants and burning them at the stake. When Mary also died young, Lady Jane Grey, another Catholic, reluctantly succeeded to the throne, but was deposed and executed within a matter of days. Elizabeth, as the last of the king's surviving children and a staunch Protestant, like her father, then became Queen of England, on 17 November 1558.

There were many who were ready to criticise the new queen, and she certainly had her faults: she was vain, bad-tempered and impatient, and could be extremely over-dramatic and neurotic. She had inherited her mother's good looks, passionate nature and love of sumptuous clothing and jewellery; from her father came her flaming red hair and irascible temper. However, despite the young queen's failings, she went on to become one of the most popular monarchs the country had ever known. She proved deeply committed to the task of

Seen here at her coronation in 1558, Elizabeth I, 'the Virgin Queen', ruled England during a period of incredible turmoil

After the death of Mary – pictured here with Lord Darnley, her husband – Elizabeth was wracked with guilt and paranoia

ruling England, showing her affection for its people openly, often making tours or 'progresses' around the country to show off her wealth, and keep in touch with the populace. She also made rousing public speeches to gain popularity among the common folk, especially at times of war (a practice unheard of for women at the time). She was a clever woman, with a quick intelligence that probably helped keep her alive at a time when plots against the monarchy were a daily threat. Moreover, she had the sense to surround herself with loyal, experienced ministers who would stop at nothing to ensure that she stayed on the throne, using any means – including espionage, torture and murder – to keep the queen safe from her many would-be assassins.

Murdered in an explosion

On her accession to the throne, Elizabeth made religious tolerance a priority. She returned the country to the Protestant faith, but – despite criticism from puritanical sects – ensured that some of the trappings of the Catholic faith, such as candles and incense, were retained in church worship. In this way, she managed to tread an uneasy path of compromise throughout her reign, keeping the Protestant and Catholic elements of the church in relative harmony, although at times this seemed almost impossible. One of the main stumbling blocks to this tenuous balance was Mary, Queen of Scots, the daughter of James V of Scotland, who wanted to seize the throne and return England to the Catholic faith.

Mary, Queen of Scots, had been born in Scotland in 1542, and had spent her early years there with her mother, a Frenchwoman. She then went to live at the French court, and eventually became queen of France, but only for a few months, as her husband, Francis II, died young. She returned to Scotland as queen, although the Protestants there regarded her with great suspicion and made her promise to respect their religion publicly while practising her own privately. She remarried, this time to Lord Darnley, who proved a violent, unreliable husband. In 1566, Darnley stabbed Mary's secretary, David Riccio, to death, and was later murdered himself, in an explosion at his house. Rumours spread that Mary had been responsible for Darnley's murder. Also accused was Mary's third husband, the Earl of Bothwell, whom she had married only a few weeks after Darnley's death. Becoming more and more unpopular with the Scots, Mary was eventually deposed and imprisoned at Lochleven Castle.

Mary taken prisoner

However, Mary was determined to keep up her fight to protect the Catholic faith, and her supporters continued to dispute Elizabeth's claim to the English throne (as Elizabeth had been declared illegitimate at one time). Mary escaped from her imprisonment in Scotland, dressed as a man, and travelled to England, hoping to meet Elizabeth and put her case. However, Elizabeth's advisers knew that Mary was a serious threat to the English throne; there were many Catholics in the country who saw her as the rightful queen of England. Instead of going to meet Mary in person, Elizabeth sent one of her ministers, and Mary was

The beheading of Mary, Queen of Scots, came about after Elizabeth discovered she had been involved in a plot against her

taken to stay in Tutbury Castle. After weeks of waiting for an audience with the queen, Mary realized that she had been taken prisoner.

Elizabeth, for her part, became more and more agitated about what to do. She wanted to visit Mary, partly out of sheer curiosity, since Mary was said to be a fascinating woman, like herself.

However, Elizabeth knew that to strike up a relationship with Mary would be to court danger, which was the last thing she wanted to do in her precarious position.

Meanwhile, a group of Catholic aristocrats tried to rescue Mary from her imprisonment, but the plot failed. Another plan by Spanish aristocrats to get rid of Elizabeth and replace her on the throne with Mary, the Ridolfi Plot of 1571, also failed.

Then came evidence that Mary herself was involved in a plot to kill Queen Elizabeth. One of the key queen's ministers, Francis Walsingham, discovered that Mary had been corresponding with a group of Catholics who wanted Elizabeth out of the way, and cleverly found out who the plotters were by forging a note, purporting to be from Mary, asking for the identities of the men. Like lambs to the slaughter, the plotters sent in the names, and Walsingham finally had the evidence he needed to arrest Mary and charge her with treason.

Botched execution job

At her trial on 15 October 1586, Mary was forbidden to employ a counsel for the defence, was swiftly convicted of treason, and then sentenced to death. All that remained was for Queen Elizabeth to sign the death warrant, but to her advisers' dismay, Elizabeth could not bring herself to do so. She was particularly anxious about executing a woman who, like herself, was a queen.

She procrastinated for weeks, which infuriated her ministers, but eventually agreed to sign the warrant. After the deed was done, Elizabeth became distraught, and appeared to bitterly regret her decision. Her anguish was made worse by reports that, when Mary was beheaded, the executioner had botched the job and had had to make several cuts before the head came off cleanly. In a further macabre detail, it was said that when the executioner held Mary's head up by the hair for the people present to see, he was left holding her wig, while the head rolled off on to the floor, the lips still moving in prayer.

Fury provoked

The execution of Mary, Queen of Scots, may have got rid of one of Elizabeth's main enemies, but it provoked fury among the many Catholic countries of Europe. Only a year later, the Spanish Armada was assembled to fight against the English. The British defeated the Spanish, but hostilities between the British and Spanish went on for many years after that. The years that followed also saw warfare between Britain and Ireland. In addition, the queen's spirits began to decline, partly because of the deaths of loyal friends such as Walsingham and the Earl of Leicester, and partly because constant political pressures began to take their toll. On 24 March 1603, the queen, now troubled by ill health, the question of her successor and anxiety about being assassinated, finally died.

Golden age

'Good Queen Bess', as she had become known, was greatly mourned by the English people. Today, she is remembered as one of England's greatest monarchs. The Elizabethan era is also represented as a golden age of art, culture, exploration around the globe and political stability – even though, in fact, there were many insecurities during Elizabeth's reign, and she was in many ways a capricious ruler whose reluctance to make difficult decisions caused many problems for the future, in particular regarding England's relationships with Ireland and Spain.

However, Elizabeth's spirited attitude, her passionate attachment to the people of her country, and her canny ability to survive despite repeated assassination attempts, has made her one of the best-loved, flamboyant and memorable figures in English history.

When Elizabeth came to the throne in 1558, England was impoverished and beset with problems caused by widespread religious divisions. By the time she died in 1603, it had become one of the most prosperous and powerful countries in the world, proof if any were needed that a woman could lead the country as well as any man – if not better. Elizabeth had triumphed over adversity and her problematic birthright.

Fidel Castro looks highly amused at a newspaper report detailing an assassination attempt on his life organized in the USA

FIDEL CASTRO

Fidel Castro, the famous Cuban leader who transformed his country from an American outpost of capitalism into the first Communist state in the West, has been the subject of numerous assassination attempts. Amazingly, he has so far managed to escape death, even though many of his enemies, reportedly including the CIA, have plotted to assassinate him. Yet, through a combination of good luck and high security measures, not to mention bungling incompetence on the part of his many would-be assassins, Castro has continued to survive despite the odds, and to this day, as an octogenarian, he continues to remain in power.

Revolution and Cold War

Fidel Alejandro Castro Ruz was born on 13 August 1926, and grew up under the regime of Fulgencio Batista in Cuba. As a student, he became active in politics, denouncing the regime, which he and many others considered to be corrupt and over-dependent on US corporate finance. In 1953, he led an attack on the army, which resulted in his exile from Cuba. Not deterred, he returned in December 1956 with a guerrilla force and invaded the country. In 1959, he gained power, and began to revolutionize the Cuban economy with a series of Marxist-oriented programmes for improved state education and health. Since that time, his regime has implemented many radical programmes in Cuba, such as free healthcare, free education, nationalization of major industries, collectivization of agriculture and extensive land reform. Many admire what he has done for the poorer elements of Cuban society; however, he also has many critics, especially in the United States, whose economic and political interests in the country were severely damaged when Castro took over. Critics of the regime also point to the fact that, over the years, Castro has become an autocratic ruler, to the point of being a dictator, and that the economy of Cuba is still in a parlous state.

After Castro's successful revolt against the Batista regime in 1959, he encountered two major opponents to his new regime: the United States government, and the Mafia, whose business interests of gambling, drug running and prostitution, were irreparably damaged. Amid the paranoia of the Cold War in the 1950s and 60s, the US government and its security arm, the CIA, felt entitled to do everything in their power to rid itself of the Communist threat in their back yard. The Cuban Missile Crisis of 1962, in which the Soviets planned to arm Cuba with nuclear weapons, caused a clash of world powers to the point where nuclear war became a distinct possibility, only averted at the last minute, thus revealing just how tense relations between the West and the East had become.

Behind the scenes plots

In this climate of distrust, the Eisenhower and Kennedy administrations considered it a matter of national security to undermine Castro's communist regime in Cuba, and in so doing to restore America's influence there. Thus, numerous ideas as to how to assassinate or discredit Castro were devised,

A rare photograph of Castro taken in 1957 for a CBS report on Cuba's jungle fighters before the Batista government fell

which were later described in a CIA document, 'The Inspector General's Report on Plots to Assassinate Fidel Castro', which was made public under a programme of historical review. Some of it makes such bizarre reading it is hard to believe CIA operatives really came up with such plans; however, in the context of other CIA initiatives at the period, such as their experimentation with mind-altering drugs under the 'MKULTRA' programme, it does seem that they have some basis in historical reality.

First, the plots to discredit Castro. These included contaminating the booth where the President made his speeches on the radio with a chemical similar to LSD, sprayed into the air via an aerosol canister. The idea was that Castro would become high, start talking gobbledegook and make an idiot of himself, thus losing the respect of the population as he babbled nonsensically on air. However, the plan was abandoned when it was decided by technicians that the results of the spray were unpredictable.

Exploding cigars

Next, the CIA came up with the idea of contaminating a box of Castro's famous cigars, soaking them in a chemical that would have the same effect. According to this plan, Castro would smoke one of these cigars before addressing the population, and proceed to talk complete rubbish, once again discrediting himself. And, as if that were not enough, there was also a scheme to contaminate cigars with a chemical to make Castro's beard fall out, the idea being that, without his beard, Castro would immediately be seen as a figure of fun. Another idea was to put a thallium powder into Castro's shoes when he put them out at night to be cleaned. The powder would also have the effect of making Castro lose his beard hair.

In retrospect, one cannot help wondering if the CIA operatives who came up with such ideas had themselves been partaking of the psychotropic drugs they were considering using to discredit Castro; however, it seems that someone had enough sense to abandon such plans, as they were never put into practice. Chief J. D. Esterline of the CIA later admitted that the agency could not work out a way to deliver the cigars safely into the hands of Castro's aides, and realised that if their schemes were discovered, they, rather than Castro, would be made to look foolish. Accordingly, the box of cigars was destroyed, and other ideas explored.

Lethal poison

Next, instead of making Castro look a fool, the CIA looked at ways of assassinating him. Dr Edward Gunn, who worked in the medical divison, reported that he received a box of Castro's favourite brand of cigars, and was asked to treat them with a lethal substance. A member of the technical division also remembered lacing a box of fifty cigars with a toxin called botulinum, which would act as a lethal poison, killing the president. A cigar from the box was later tested, and was found to have so much of the toxin in it that it would have killed Castro even if he had just put it in his mouth, let alone smoked it.

Other methods of poisoning Castro were also considered, such as using shellfish poison to contaminate his food, or soaking one of his handkerchiefs, cups of coffee or cigars with lethal bacteria in liquid form. Alternatively, a 'lethal pill' could be used, again containing botulinum. In order to test the effectiveness of the pills, the technical department bought some guinea pigs and gave them some, but to their surprise, the guinea pigs survived. The team surmised that the guinea pigs had some immunity to the pills, and tried them on monkeys, with better results.

Having found the method they wanted to use, the CIA operatives arranged for the pills to be secretly delivered to Castro, hidden in a pencil, through their Mafia connections. However, Juan Orta, a Castro aide who was in league with the Mafia men, and who was supposed to administer the poison by slipping a pill into Castro's drink, was sacked from his job at the last minute, and the plan misfired.

Sick of trying to poison Castro by covert means, the agency investigated the possibility of a good, old-fashioned drive-by killing, to be performed by their Mafia friends in Cuba. However, Mafia boss Sam Giancana refused to take on the job, pointing out that there would be very few gunmen prepared to attempt to kill the president, who was constantly surrounded by security men. Their chances of escaping from the scene of the crime, he thought, would be virtually nil.

Contaminated diving suit

The United States' attempt to overthrow Castro in the Bay of Pigs invasion of 1961 for a while distracted attention away from these assassination plots – why make secret plans to get rid of the president when armed men were doing their best to overthrow his regime in broad daylight? However, when the attempted invasion failed, the pressure to assassinate Castro was on again, and this time the CIA came up with a new idea – the contaminated skin diving suit.

According to this plan, which seemed even more bizarre than previous ones, Castro, a keen skin diver, was to be presented with a new suit, inside which was a lethal dusting powder. The powder would infect him with a fungus known as 'Madura foot', which would cause him a dreadful skin disease. Not only this, tuberculosis bacteria would also be put inside the suit. The man who would be given the task of presenting the suit, as a gift, would be attorney James Donovan, who had been involved in negotiating the return of prisoners from the Bay of Pigs invasion with Castro. Unfortunately for the CIA, and fortunately for Castro, it turned out that Donovan had coincidentally already given Castro a diving suit as a gift. Once again, the plan had to be abandoned.

After this, the CIA continued to think up ways of getting rid of Castro, from devious poisoning plots to overt shoot-outs in public, but their plans were constantly foiled. In the end, it seemed that their ideas did more to damage relations between the US and the Cuban diplomatic services than anything else – not surprisingly, given this history, the Cubans came to distrust the Americans in negotiations between the two countries. And in the end, Castro survived, despite the many plans laid to assassinate him and restore America's influence in Cuba.

CHARLES DE GAULLE

The personification of modern France, Charles de Gaulle was an army officer from Lille who went on to command the Free French Forces during the Second World War, and afterwards oversaw the creation of the Fifth Republic, serving as its elected president until 1969. His presidency saw the economic reconstruction of post-war France rapidly accelerate, as well as the creation of France as an independent nuclear power, and the formation of the EEC. However, these were also turbulent times, and French society, as politically impassioned as ever, was bitterly divided over a number of issues. Political turmoil punctuated his presidency. When he came to power in 1959 guerrillas in the French colony of Algeria were already fighting a fierce war for independence, and not long before he left it, in the summer of 1968, general insurrection broke out across France itself. By the time this eminent statesman resigned the following year, he had gained an official place in the Guinness Book of Records, under 'most failed assassination attempts survived': thirty-one, in total.

The first attempt
After the Allied liberation of France, General de Gaulle made a celebratory tour of Dakar, an important Atlantic port in French West Africa. During the war it had belonged to Vichy France, and in 1940 de Gaulle had tried, unsuccessfully, to persuade it to change sides. There then followed an attempted attack in conjunction with the

British Royal Navy, which de Gaulle eventually called off, as he 'didn't want to spill the blood of Frenchmen for Frenchmen', although a lengthy naval bombardment did follow, and the episode ended up costing the lives of hundreds of men. When the general returned in peacetime, and stood to attention on the deck of the cruiser *Georges Leygues* for the *Marseillaise*, a petty officer on an upper deck felt compelled to shoulder his rifle and take aim. He was, however, knocked down and disarmed by a fellow officer before he could get off a shot. Even before he had become a politician, de Gaulle was in the firing line.

Nemesis

While de Gaulle at some point or other seemingly managed to earn the disapproval of one faction or another in France, from the militaristic far-right to the student far-left, by far the bulk of the assassination attempts against him were the work of the Organization de l'Armée Secrète, better known by its acronym the OAS. This 'Secret Army Organisation' was mostly made up of veterans from the recent war in Indochina, where military defeat at the hands of the Viet Minh had forced France to relinquish her imperial claims on the territory that was to become Cambodia, Laos and Vietnam. Disgruntled at this rolling back of the French Empire, the OAS became adamant that Algeria, annexed by France in 1834, would remain part of the republic. Although it had encountered occasional resistance from that date on, the failure of Algeria's regional government to represent the Muslim majority led to continuous armed resistance

Numerous different factions seemed to be lining up to take pot shots at de Gaulle, seen here visiting his troops in Algeria

De Gaulle and his customary Citroën 'Deese'

moments of pressure (although he himself always attributed it to the superior quality of French cars). On 8 September 1961, the OAS planted fifty kilos of 'plastique' (plastic explosives) and fifteen litres of napalm in a roadside culvert near his country home in Colombey-les-deux-Églises, and detonated it by remote control as his car, a Citroën 'Deese' (Citroën DS), approached. The explosion nearly wrenched the car off the road, but de Gaulle ordered his chauffeur to accelerate and drive directly into the flames. The car and its occupants survived intact.

By the following year attempts on the president's life had become so frequent that both de Gaulle and his wife had become almost blasé about them. When the presidential (and unarmoured) car was showered with bullets that August, by now a fairly regular occurrence, the bodyguard who accompanied them ordered them to take cover immediately, yet neither of them moved. When the car pulled to a halt a safe distance away from their attackers, de Gaulle got out and coolly dusted the broken glass off his clothing before complaining about the OAS's terrible marksmanship. Later that evening his wife was asked if she was frightened. 'Of what?' she replied. 'We'd have died together. And no old age!'

The Big One
Perhaps the most famous of all the assassination attempts on de Gaulle came only a few days later. This was the shooting on the 22 August 1962. It took place in the Petit-Clamart suburb of Paris, where a small team of assassins armed with machine guns strafed the president's unarmoured Citroën

from 1954 onwards. During this period, many hoped that de Gaulle's election in 1958 would end the bloodshed. After considering the matter, however, de Gaulle decided that further military activity in the area would not be a good idea, and called for a three-year ceasefire, to be followed by an Algerian referendum on independence. For the OAS, this was simply a countdown to defeat, and had to be stopped by any means. They embarked on a terrorist campaign to goad the Algerians into breaking the cease-fire, and planned and mounted a series of attempts to assassinate the president himself.

Grace under pressure
It has been suggested that part of the reason de Gaulle survived so many attempts on his life was because of his natural calm in

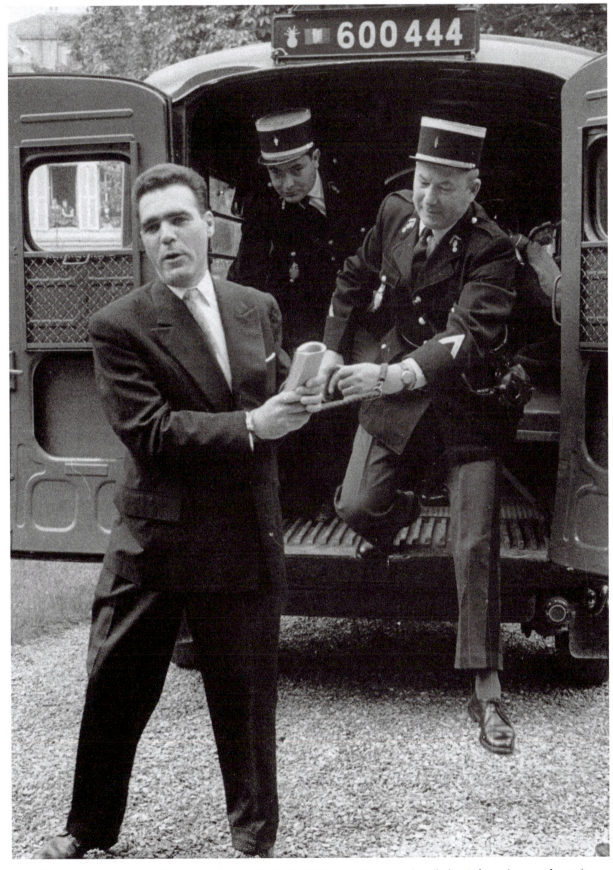

One of the suspects alleged to have been involved in the Petit-Clamart shooting is bundled out of a police van for trial

DS, in what was by now an all too familiar *modus operandi*. What was remarkable was the amount of ammunition spent: fourteen bullets hitting the car itself, with twenty hitting the café behind and an additional one hundred and eighty-seven hitting the pavement, a figure that is especially remarkable considering that de Gaulle and his entourage survived entirely unharmed. Truly, the OAS were awful shots. But the danger had been very real and de Gaulle was lucky to have escaped with his life. The Petit-Clamart attempt is probably most often remembered because its conspirators were caught and tried, amongst them the mastermind of the operation, Jean-Marie Bastien-Thiry.

Bastien-Thiry was a 36-year-old Catholic Air Force engineer who specialized in designing air-to-air missiles, and was married to the daughter of a former Vichy minister. A dedicated member of the OAS, he considered an independent Algeria to be an 'even graver loss than that of Alsace-Lorraine'. Bolstered by his reading of Thomas Aquinas's writings on regicide, he set about organizing the ambush, although not before receiving absolution from a Dominican priest. He was arrested after returning from a research trip to the UK, and claimed in court that he was only trying to prevent the 'inevitable genocide' of Europeans in Algeria that would occur if the country gained independence. He went on to compare himself to the German officers who had plotted to kill Hitler. After a psychiatric examination, he was tried by a military tribunal and sentenced to death by firing squad.

De Gaulle refused clemency, despite the best efforts of the condemned's elder brother, and cited three reasons: he had endangered the lives of bystanders innocent even by Bastien-Thiry's standards; he had involved foreigners in his plot (three Hungarians, to be precise); and he had been careful not to share the dangers to which he exposed his sub-ordinates, directing the operation from afar. In a private conversation, the president later explained, in a somewhat Gallic fashion, 'the French need martyrs...I could have given them one of those idiotic generals playing ball in Tulle prison. I gave them Bastien-Thiry. They'll be able to make a martyr of him. He deserves it.'

A ripe old age

After the independence of Algeria the attempts on de Gaulle's life tailed off. After the turbulent summer of 1968 he resigned, despite winning a massive majority in the recent elections. He declared that he had finally had enough of politics, especially French politics: how can anyone be expected to govern a country that has two hundred and forty-six different types of cheese, he once commented. He returned to the president's country house at Colombey-les-deux-Églises and set about writing his memoirs, and eventually died watching the evening news. He was eighty years of age, and unlike most other politicians, left behind a family that was not at all well-heeled. In a snub to the establishment, he kept his funeral a private, family affair in Colombey itself, and the heads of state had to content themselves with a casketless ceremony in Notre Dame. His gravestone reads simply 'Charles de Gaulle, 1890–1970'.

POPE JOHN PAUL II

Pope John Paul II, who was pope between 1978 and 2005, survived several assassination attempts during his 27-year reign. One of the most popular popes of all time, despite his conservative stance on contraception and abortion, he eventually died of Parkinson's disease, and was mourned throughout the world.

He was born Karol Jozef Wojtyla on 18 May 1920 in Wadowice, southern Poland. His father, whom he was named after, was a former army officer. According to those who knew him when he was growing up, his mother Emilia was convinced that her son, nicknamed 'Lolek', would be a great man one day, and told people so. He was brought up in a very religious household, so much so that when he was nine, on hearing that his mother had died of kidney failure and heart disease, he merely said, 'It was God's will'. A further tragedy followed when his brother Edmund died of scarlet fever.

Run over by truck

As a young man, Karol went to Krakow to study at the university, excelling as a student and learning eleven languages, most of which he spoke fluently. When Poland was occupied by the Germans during the Second World War, he and his father made a dramatic escape, walking for over a hundred miles towards Russia, only to find that Russia too had invaded their country. They were forced to return to Krakow. The university was then closed by the Nazis, and Karol found work as a restaurant messenger.

He later worked as a quarryman, all the time continuing his education as best he could. He was also engaged in undercover resistance work, helping Jews to escape from the Nazis, through a secret organization run by the former archbishop of Krakow, Cardinal Sapieha.

One day, as he was returning from work at the quarry on 29 February 1944, he was involved in an accident when a German truck ran him over. He was badly hurt, and suffered severe concussion, spending a fortnight in hospital. According to later accounts, this brush with death had a galvanizing effect on the young man: he vowed to become a priest and dedicate his life to God.

Escape from the Gestapo

This was a turbulent time in Poland, and in August 1944 an armed struggle of Poles to liberate the nation from Nazi rule began. The Warsaw Uprising, as it was known, spread to Krakow, and was brutally suppressed by the Gestapo, who tried to round up all young men to prevent them joining the resistance. The Gestapo called on Wojtyla and searched the house, but he managed to hide, and escaped to the protection of the archbishop, where he remained for the rest of the war.

The year after the war ended, in 1946, Wojtyla was ordained a priest and went to Rome to begin his ecclesiastical studies. He met students from all over the world, and wrote a thesis on the concept of faith in the teaching of St John of the Cross. On completion of his training, his first job was as pastor of a village called Niegowic, outside Krakow. At the same time, he began a religious group called 'Rodzinka', the little family, who would meet to pray and talk. As the group grew larger, Wojtyla organized sporting trips, where the discussions continued. He was also busy writing poems and plays, published under pseudonyms. His career prospered, and in 1958, he was ordained as the youngest bishop in Poland. By 1963, he was archbishop of Krakow, and then became a cardinal. In August 1978, he was ordained as Pope John Paul II.

Three shots fired

The first attempt on his life came on the afternoon of 13 May 1981 as he entered St Peter's Square to address a crowd of twenty thousand people who had gathered there to hear him. His open-topped car was moving slowly along, when three bullets were fired, two of them striking the pope. He was immediately rushed to hospital, where he underwent a critical six-hour operation. Two members of the crowd were also injured.

A bystander caught the assassin before he could run away, and the police then arrested him. The assassin turned out to be a 23-year-old Turkish terrorist, Mehmet Ali Agca. When he was picked up, some notes were found in his pocket, indicating that he belonged to a group called the Grey Wolves, a far-right Turkish terrorist group. However, Agca claimed that he was acting alone, even though there were reports that another man had been seen running away from the square when the shooting occurred.

Agca was brought to trial, convicted of the crime, and sentenced to prison. The pope visited his assailant while he was in prison, and later said that he had pardoned him. A

As the pope entered St Peter's Square on 13 May 1981, he was hit by two bullets. The gunman's hand is circled

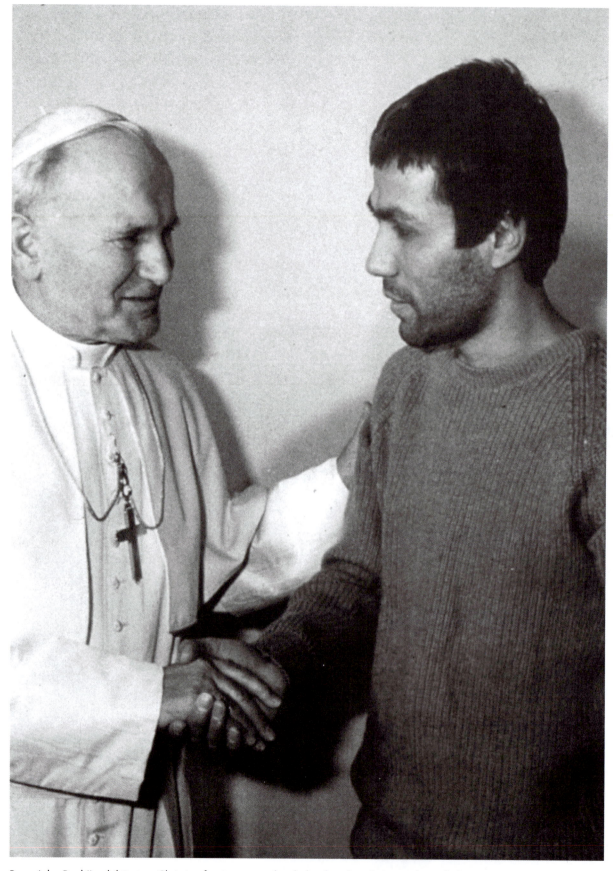

Pope John Paul II exhibits true Christian forgiveness as he shakes hands with Agca, the Turkish terrorist who tried to kill him

theory later arose that Agca had been acting at the behest of the Soviet Union and the Bulgarian secret service, who viewed John Paul II as a threat to communism. An investigation was launched, and a group of Bulgarians and Turks were arrested and brought to trial. However, the case fell apart when Agca came to testify, and it became clear that he was not altogether sane – at one point he claimed that he was Jesus Christ. Also, the CIA evidence linking him to the Communist authorities turned out to be somewhat dubious.

The Grey Wolves

It never became entirely clear why Agca had made the assassination attempt, but it seems that his motivations were a combination of political beliefs and mental imbalance. He had been born in a village called Ismailli in the Malatya province of Turkey, and as a young man had joined a street gang and turned to petty crime. After making a living for a while as a smuggler between Turkey and Bulgaria, he went to Syria to train as a terrorist for the Palestinians, which he claimed was paid for by the Bulgarian government. On his return to Turkey, he began to work for the neofascist terrorist organization The Grey Wolves, who some believe were being funded by the CIA to destabilize the country, leading to a military coup there in 1980. (Others believe that the Bulgarian secret service were behind the organization.)

On 1 February 1979, Agca murdered the editor of a centre left newspaper, Abdi Ipekci, in Istanbul. He was caught and convicted of the crime, but only served a few months of his sentence before escaping to Bulgaria. He then began to travel around the Mediterranean, and came to Italy in 1981, where he met up with accomplices to plan the assassination of the pope.

The Pilgrim Pope

There were more attempts on the pope's life in later years, including one incident in Portugal in which a man tried to stab him with a bayonet but was prevented from doing so by security guards. This time, the would-be assassin was a priest, Juan Maria Fernandez y Krohn, who considered the pope to be a Soviet agent. Krohn was arrested, brought to trial, convicted and given a six-year sentence. He was also forced to leave the priesthood and exiled from his country.

Despite these threats to his life, and his own failing health, Pope John Paul went on to complete the second longest reign ever as pope, remaining in office for twenty-seven years. He was a traditionalist, speaking out against contraception, abortion and scientific intervention in the process of human reproduction. He opposed homosexuality and same-sex marriage, and was a stern critic of divorce. He also opposed the ordination of women to the priesthood in the church. He was against euthanasia. For these reasons, many considered him to be reactionary, and felt that he had done much to hold back progress in Catholic countries where poverty and over-population were serious problems, particularly impacting on women. On the other hand, the pope was highly critical of repressive ideologies, both on the left and the right, and denounced the excesses of western capitalism, believing that its materialistic values of greed and unrestrained consumerism were at the heart of many modern ills.

The pope also travelled constantly, building links between the church and organizations in many countries, so much so that he became known as the 'Pilgrim Pope'. He also canonized over a thousand saints from many different backgrounds, in this way bringing a wider variety of cultures and nationalities to the religion of Catholicism. Thus, whatever his true legacy, for most of his reign he fulfilled his role in an extremely active way, bringing the Catholic church back to the fore of contemporary life, carving out a role in which the church constantly engaged with, and commented on, the problems of the modern world, instead of attempting to remain aloof from them.

Assassin's good wishes

In his old age, the pope contracted Parkinson's disease, but continued to remain in office, despite calls that he should resign and let someone younger and fitter get on with the job. On 2 April 2005, he finally died. Huge crowds all over the world turned out to mourn his passing, and he has since been referred to among Catholics, including his successor Pope Benedict XVI, as 'John Paul the Great'.

In a curious postscript to the assassination affair, during the pope's last illness, Mehmet Ali Agca sent him a letter wishing him well. He also warned the pope that the end of the world was nigh. After the pope's death, Agca's brother Adnan gave an interview in which he stated that the Agca family were in

deep mourning, and considered the pope their friend. Mehmet Ali, now imprisoned in Turkey, asked to be allowed to attend the pope's funeral, but the Turkish authorities wisely forbade that he should be released.

RONALD REAGAN

Many presidents of the United States have suffered assassination attempts. Some of these have been fatal – the presidents who were killed are Abraham Lincoln in 1865, James Garfield in 1881, William McKinley in 1901, and John F. Kennedy in 1963. Other presidents have been lucky enough to escape with their lives: Andrew Jackson in 1835, Theodore Roosevelt in 1912, Franklin D. Roosevelt in 1933, Harry S. Truman in 1950, Gerald Ford in 1975 and Ronald Reagan in 1981. In some cases, the fact that the attempt was foiled was the result of tight security measures; in others, sheer chance had a role to play. The US Secret Service Division began in 1865 with the aim of suppressing counterfeit currency. After the assassination of McKinley, Congress informally requested Secret Service protection for the president and in 1902 the Secret Service assumed responsibility for the president's safety, with two operatives assigned full time to the White House. In later years, protection was extended to the immediate family of the president, the vice president and former presidents as well as visiting heads of state.

Certainly, in recent years, particularly following the increase in terrorist attacks, the security surrounding the president of the United States has become much tighter, so

Assassination attempts seem almost to go with the job of being US President. Here, Ronald Reagan makes a speech in California

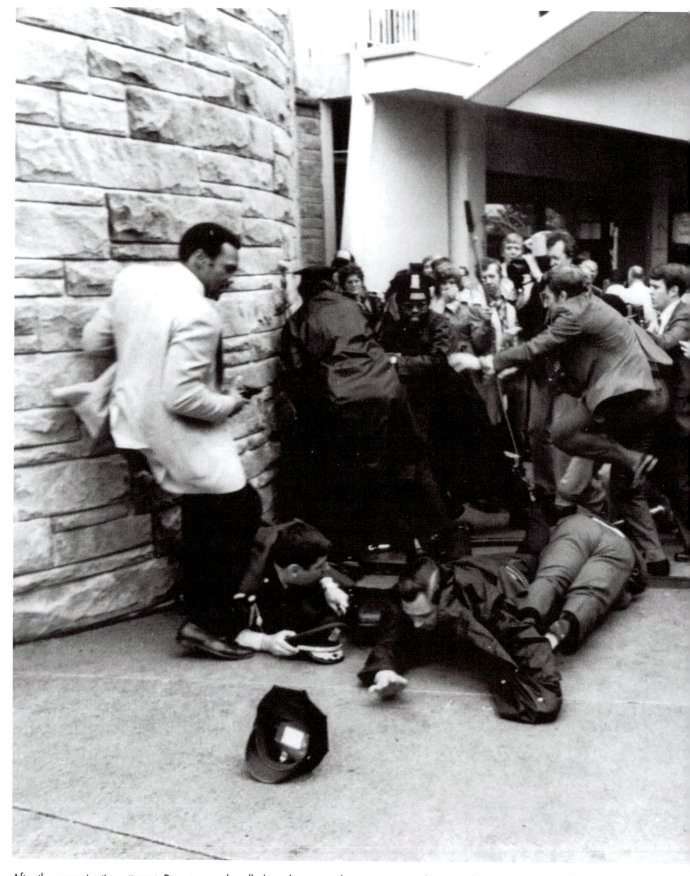

After the assassination attempt, Reagan was bundled into his car and was not aware that any of the bullets had touched him

that the chances of a future assassination attempt are much lower. Having said that, it is always impossible to guarantee one hundred per cent security for the president, especially when so much of the presidential role is a public one, addressing huge crowds and travelling around the country constantly. The security forces have always to tread a fine line between making sure safety is of the highest standard, and ensuring that the president is able to keep in touch with the citizens of the country at first hand, whether the occasions be huge rallies or small, intimate gatherings.

Lone gunman

In the case of Ronald Reagan, whose presidency lasted through most of the 1980s, from 1981 to 1989, the assassination attempt was so confusing that the president himself did not realize he had been shot until he was in his car. As he reached the car, a hail of bullets were fired, but Reagan was not aware that any of the bullets had touched him. He merely thought that he had been injured as a result of the fact that a security agent, realizing what was going on, roughly shoved him into the presidential car.

The assassination attempt came on 30 March 1981, and was the work of a mentally unbalanced drifter, John W. Hinckley. Hinckley had been inspired to kill the president after watching the film *Taxi Driver*, in which a lone gunman tries to kill a presidential candidate. (Ironically, the film had been based on the case of Arthur Bremer, an assassin who had attempted to kill Governor George Wallace on 15 May 1972. Wallace had been left permanently paralyzed as a result of the attempt, and several other aides had been wounded. Bremer was sentenced to 63 years imprisonment for the shooting.)

The shooting

On the fatal day in question, Hinckley, a native of Evergreen, Colorado, waited for Reagan to leave the Washington Hilton Hotel, where he had been giving a speech. He used a revolver to fire five or six shots at the president, hitting him under the arm, so that the bullet ricocheted off him, then passed between his ribs and into part of his lung. When he was hit, the president stopped still for a moment, and was pushed into the waiting car. He did not realize what had happened, and had not felt the bullet pass into his body. However, he began to feel ill, so ordered the car to take him to hospital. It was only on the way that it was found that he had been wounded in the shooting.

Also injured at the scene were his press secretary, James S. Brady, who was shot in the head; a secret service agent named Timothy J. McCarthy; and Timothy K. Delahanty, a police officer. They all recovered, except Brady who was permanently impaired by the shooting. In later years, Brady became an enthusiastic supporter of tightening up the gun control laws in the USA. Reagan himself continued to defend the rights of US citizens to own and use guns, despite the fact that he and his aides had almost been killed by a lone gunman who was mentally out of control.

The assassin, John Hinckley, was soon caught and arrested. During his trial, it turned out that he was the son of a well-to-do oil executive. He had had a privileged childhood, living first in Dallas, and then moving to Colorado. He became interested in far-right politics as a student, joining the National Socialist Party, otherwise known as the Nazi party, in 1978. He was known to have a violent temper, and had his membership cancelled a year after joining the party. He then had some brushes with the law, including an incident in 1980 when he was arrested at the airport in Nashville, Tennessee, with three guns and a stash of ammunition in his luggage. This was revealed by an X-ray machine. It just so happened that President Jimmy Carter was in Nashville that day, and it seems likely that John Hinckley had followed him there. He was given a small fine and let go a few days later, whereupon he bought some more guns, one of which he later used to shoot President Reagan.

Love letter

It was then discovered that only hours before he made the assassination attempt, Hinckley had written a love letter to film star Jodie Foster. In it, he explained how he wanted to kill the president for her sake, and that he was doing it as a way of showing how much he loved her. Clearly, he was mentally unbalanced and, when he was brought to trial, it was assumed that he was acting alone. However, William Casey, boss of the CIA, feared the Soviets may have had a hand in the killing – Reagan was one of the most openly anti-Communist presidents of the US for many years. However, after a detailed investigation, the idea that Hinckley was working for the KGB was ruled out.

Nazi sympathizer John Hinckley Jr pictured outside the White House: he was obsessed with the film star Jodie Foster

Because of Hinckley's unbalanced state of mind, the jury ruled that he was not guilty of the crime, but rather that he was insane, and should be incarcerated in a mental institution. The verdict deeply shocked American citizens, many of whom felt that the perpetrator of such a crime should be imprisoned. It only became clear in later years that Reagan had almost died as a result of the shooting, and that he had been seriously ill afterwards. He had pretended to be fine directly after the event, and had continued to present himself as completely recovered, but the truth was that the injury had affected his breathing and concentration, to the point where he often became disoriented.

Acting

A former film actor, Reagan did a good job of covering up his real condition, but the event was certainly far more significant than had at first been thought. Had this been known at the time, it is possible that Hinckley would have received a prison sentence, rather than an order to be detained in a mental institution.

One of the reasons it was so important for Reagan to come over as invincible was that, during the 1980s, he was trying to restore faith in the idea of a strong nation with a strong leader at its head. He had defeated President Jimmy Carter at the beginning of the decade, and had ushered in a new era of what was called 'Reaganomics' – with the emphasis on free enterprise, lower spending on welfare, cuts in income tax, and so on. While many saw Reagan as damaging the egalitarian social structure of America,

particularly in ignoring the needs of the poor, others felt that he had restored optimism to the nation, emphasizing traditional values and making America 'great again'.

The Reagan regime was arguably a factor in the eventual collapse of Soviet Communism, and he is also credited as the founder of a new conservative movement in America that continues to this day. Certainly, his approach was welcomed by a large proportion of the electorate at the time; he was re-elected after his first term of office with a landslide victory. During his presidency, he was seen as a popular figure with a unique ability to communicate with the public, emphasizing the folksy, downhome nature of his political viewpoint; however, there were also many who criticized him, pointing to the selfish values of the prevailing entrepreneurial ethos, which they felt undermined the social fabric of a community-based culture. Moreover, Reagan's ability to understand the complex issues of politics and government was also questioned, especially as he got older and more absent-minded.

Reagan had an uncanny ability to survive political scandals and come out smelling of roses. During his presidency, a number of administration officials and staff were convicted of crimes but none of this seemed to impact on Reagan, which is why he was given the nickname 'the Teflon President'.

Despite his brush with death in 1981, Reagan went on to live a long life, dying at his home in Bel-Air, California, aged 93, after suffering from Alzheimer's disease for the last ten years of his life. He was awarded a state funeral.

KING HUSSEIN

King Hussein, the ruler of Jordan from 1952 until 1992, managed to stay on the throne for many years despite living through extremely turbulent times. Indeed, he only came to the throne as a result of the assassination of his grandfather, King Abdullah I, and narrowly escaped assassination himself when the king was killed. For his admirers, King Hussein is seen as a great statesman, whose diplomatic skills protected Jordan from her many enemies during a time of great political conflict between the Israelis and Arabs, which included both open warfare and guerrilla conflict.

His critics, however, see King Hussein as an opportunist, who betrayed the Arab cause by dealing separately with Israel to further Jordan's interests, as well as the interests of the threatened Jordanian monarchy, at the expense of the Arab world in general, and of the many Palestinians living in Jordan in particular.

Three fatal bullets

King Hussein's eventful life as a monarch began on 20 July 1951, when he travelled with his grandfather, King Abdullah I, to a public place of worship in Jerusalem. As they climbed the steps of the mosque to join in the prayers, a gunman fired three bullets at King Abdullah, which hit him in the head and the chest, killing him. The young Hussein was also a target, standing by as his grandfather lay bleeding next to him. However, Hussein was saved by a medal that he was wearing,

given to him as a gift by his grandfather. The bullet aimed at the young man struck the medal on his chest and ricocheted off, wounding him slightly but saving his life.

Only a few days before the shooting, the prime minister of Lebanon, Riad Bey al-Solh, had been assassinated in Amman. Many believed that the prime minister had been killed because he had been at the forefront of peace discussions with Israel, separately from the rest of the Arab world. Jordan had also been involved in the plans. It was also well known that King Abdullah was a moderate man, with a relatively pro-Western outlook, who looked favourably on making peace with Israel, and was seemingly ready to sign an accord with the Israelis in the near future. Thus, King Abdullah became a target as well.

Anti-Zionist conspiracy

Ironically, King Abdullah had in fact travelled to Jerusalem with his grandson Hussein for the purpose of giving a eulogy at the funeral of Riad Bey al-Solh, the Lebanese prime minister.

While in the city, he had gone to the mosque with his grandson to perform his Friday prayers, along with his security men, who were always in attendance with him. However, the gunman who shot him had somehow managed to break through the security arrangements. After the shooting, the gunman was immediately arrested and was later identified as Mustapha Shukri Usho, a Palestinian tailor. Usho was living and working in Jerusalem, and was a member of the Arab Dynamite Squad. This was an organization committed to continuing hostilities with the Israelis, and dedicated to the restoration of territory to the Palestinians.

It was found that Usho had not been acting on his own, but had committed the crime at the behest of Colonel Abdullah Tell, an ex-military governor of Jerusalem, and another Arab activist, Dr Musa Abdullah Husseini. Moreover, it later transpired that Tell had ordered the execution of the gunman after he had done the deed, so that the conspirators behind the plot – himself and Husseini – would not be found. After the assassination, Tell and Husseini escaped to Egypt, where they were given protection by supporters of their cause. They were also found to be in close contact with adherents of the former 'Grand Mufti' of Jerusalem, an extreme anti-Zionist named Amin al-Husayni, who had been involved in a great deal of Muslim activism. Meanwhile, back in Amman, the investigation trail led to four co-conspirators, who were arrested, tried, convicted and sentenced to death.

After the death of King Abdullah, the next monarch on the throne was his son Talal. However, although Talal had been crowned king, he was not up to the job, since he was mentally ill, having been diagnosed with schizophrenia. He reigned from 20 July 1951 until 11 August 1952, when he was forced to abdicate the throne. However, during his brief reign, he is thought to have done a great deal to bring progress to Jordan, liberalizing the constitution, and helping to calm relations between Jordan and other Arab states such as Egypt and Saudi Arabia.

After Talal's abdication, his eldest son Hussein was formally crowned King of

March 1971 and King Hussein visits troops on the front line where tension had recently increased between Egypt and Jordan

Taking time off from all the problems of state, King Hussein relaxes with two of his children at Aqaba in Jordan

Jordan. At the time, he was only sixteen, but he did not actually begin to rule as monarch until he was eighteen.

Controversial reign

King Hussein went on to become one of Jordan's longest serving rulers. However, his reign was controversial. Jordan became one of the Arab states to continue friendly relations with the West, and was seen by western powers as a beacon of hope for settling the Israeli/Arab conflict. But it was also the case that his pro-western stance alienated Arabs in his own country, especially the many Palestinians there, who in fact formed the majority of the population.

The Palestinians not only threatened Israel's interests, but also those of the Jordanian monarchy, who were concerned to quell their claims for political sovereignty. Conflict between the monarchy and the Palestinians escalated, especially after the events of so-called 'Black September', when the Palestine Liberation Organisation was expelled from the country.

Not only did relations between the Palestinians and the Jordanian monarchy deteriorate under the leadership of King Hussein, but there were also problems between Jordan and the western world. In particular, King Hussein alienated the western powers when he formed an alliance with Saddam Hussein of Iraq in the Gulf War. By this time it was clear that King Hussein always pursued a policy of what was best for Jordan. This was understandable, and in many ways pragmatic, given the fact that his country was beset by so many enemies, but it meant that to some degree Jordan became isolated, distrusted by both western and Arabic nations.

In 1994, Jordan and Israel concluded a peace treaty that King Hussein had been working on for many years, since the 1970s. According to some commentators, this took place because the king warned the Israelis of an attack just before the Yom Kippur War. It was claimed that Hussein was seeking a special relationship with the Israelis so that his country would be able to call on their help in the event of war with Syria or Iraq. However, there were also those that discounted this theory.

Miraculous escape

Not surprisingly, given the events that led up to his reign, tight security was at the top of the agenda during his regime. In 1970, King Hussein survived an assassination attempt as he was driving in a motorcade near his summer palace, in the town of Sweileh, twelve miles from the capital city, Amman. Gunmen opened fire on the motorcade, but the king was not harmed. However, his driver was wounded. It was alleged that the king jumped out of his car and fired back at the gunmen, but this report was not substantiated.

The attack took place at a time of civil disturbance in and around Amman, as Palestinian guerrillas fought with Jordanian troops. Four hundred people were thought to have lost their lives in the conflict, as Palestinian gunmen took over the city centre and the main routes out of it.

There was even fighting at the airport, where Palestinian gunmen opened fire on the ground. The Palestinians blamed the Jordanian army for the hostilities, complaining that the army had launched attacks on Palestinian refugee camps. These had been set up after the 1967 war with Israel, in which Jordan lost the West Bank of the Jordan River to Israel, and thousands of Palestinian refugees came to Jordan to settle in the camps.

Once again, King Hussein had miraculously survived an assassination attack and escaped with his life. This time, he was not even injured. He continued to rule Jordan until 1992, enjoying his hobbies of flying aeroplanes, both propeller and jet, and amateur radio operation. He also married four times, and fathered thirteen children. Eventually, he was forced to retire from his duties as monarch due to ill health. For a number of years, he had suffered from non-Hodgkin's lymphoma, a type of cancer of the blood, and had often visited the United States for specialist treatment. He eventually died from the disease on 7 February 1999. Just before he died, he changed the constitution of the kingdom of Jordan so that his son Abdullah, rather than his brother Hassan, who was due to inherit the throne, could become ruler of the country instead. Abdullah was the son of his second wife, Princess Muna, born Antoinette Gardiner, an Englishwoman who was the daughter of an army officer

Constant threat

The choice of King Abdullah II, who was crowned after his father died, was not popular in Jordan, because his mother had been British. (The Jordanians traced the Arab lineage of their kings back to the prophet Mohammed.) Moreover, since he took over, his reign has been criticized as illiberal, since it is now forbidden to speak out against the monarch or his government's policies in Jordan. The penalties for doing so include imprisonment and heavy fines. As a result, free speech has been severely curtailed in the country, and many media and union workers have received jail sentences. King Abdullah has also been criticized for violating human rights, and has been accused of torturing dissidents, especially Islamic activists. However, his supporters point to the fact that, under the new king, the country's economy has made progress.

Like his father, King Abdullah has been known to take on the idea of disguising himself so that he can move about in public and find out what is really going on in the streets and fields of the country. According to some reports, King Hussein often disguised himself as a taxi cab driver, talking to ordinary people about the political situation as he drove them to their destinations, so as to find out how people felt about his regime. His son has also adopted this strategy at times, and in this way both kings have sought to keep in touch with the population, while avoiding the constant threat of assassination that has hung over the dynasty since the killing of King Abdullah I all those years ago.

ANDY WARHOL

On 3 June 1968, the famous pop artist Andy Warhol became the victim of an assassination attempt. Valerie Solanas, a feminist writer, came into Warhol's studio at his multi-media headquarters, the Factory, and shot him at close range. The attack almost killed him, but he survived, and later often joked about the incident. However, it was a frightening episode which revealed a darker side to the artistic New York milieu of which both she and Warhol were a part.

Andy Warhol was born Andrew Warhola in Forest City, Pennsylvania, into a working-class immigrant family. His parents, Ondrej Warhola and Julia Zavacky, were Rusyns (an ethnic minority group) from Slovakia. Ondrej worked in the Pennsylvanian coal mines. His parents were Catholics, but there were also Jewish members of the Warhola family. Early on, their son Andrew showed a strong talent as an artist, and was able to gain entry to university in Pittsburg to study commercial art. There, he developed many skills at drawing and painting, and after moving to New York City in 1949, began to work as a magazine illustrator and in advetising.

He was able to work in many styles, but in particular his trademark pen-and-ink drawings of shoes, executed in a fanciful style, were widely admired among his contemporaries.

Production-line art

During the 1960s, Warhol went on to bring his commercial expertise into the field of high art. In so doing, he began consciously to attack the values of fine art, questioning firmly entrenched attitudes such as the belief that each artist has a unique vision, that art is to do with strong emotional expression, and that each work of art is singular and valuable in itself.

Such ideas were fundamental to the theory and practice of Western art, and were part of the expressionist movement in literature, painting, sculpture and music that had become important in the early twentieth century. Warhol challenged this approach, arguing – very controversially – that art could be mass-produced, made by hired 'art workers' in a 'factory', and that it would still have as much value as a unique painting produced by one particular artist. In fact, since his death, the extent to which he left his 'art workers' to make his art works has been questioned, and it appears that, to some degree, he exaggerated the 'production line' aspect of his work. But there is no doubt that, in an age when much creative energy was being put into advertising mass-produced goods, by presenting himself as a commercial artist with a stable of workers to do his bidding, Warhol was making important points about the changing nature of art in the modern world.

Genius or con man?

At his studio, the Factory on Union Square, New York City, Warhol created a hive of activity, in which artists and others worked on many art works, from silkscreen prints to books and films. His most famous works from this period are images of mass-produced items such as the Campbell's soup

can and the Coca Cola bottle. As well as these, he produced large-scale images of American commercial culture, such as dollar signs, celebrity figures and grocery items, transforming them into modern-day icons. He emphasized that one image or item was no more important than the other, and saw American culture as a democratic one, in which everyone was essentially levelled by the need to earn money and spend it on the same mass-produced goods.

At the same time, his attitude to his work was never very clear: his remarks on the process of making and consuming art were famously cryptic, and often very tongue-in-cheek. Indeed, throughout his entire career, he amused, confused and often angered the media and the public with his pronouncements. To his supporters, he was a fascinating figure in the modern art world; to his detractors, he was a charlatan whose main focus was on making as much money as possible, and conning the art world in the process.

In fact, Warhol was a complex individual, who on the one hand craved fame and publicity, surrounding himself with celebrities and socialites, and on the other, regularly helped out at shelters for the homeless in the city. He was a rebel, not only in his approach to art, but in his personal life – he was openly homosexual at a time when this was not at all the norm – yet, at the same time, he had a conservative streak, and was quiet and shy as a person.

His immigrant roots and the religious beliefs of his parents, coupled with his observation, education and experience as an artist, made for a fascinating blend of

Ex-prostitute and playwright Valerie Solanas fired three shots at pop artist Andy Warhol then turned her gun on a critic

tradition and innovation in his work, and today he is regarded as one of the greatest artists of the twentieth century.

Sexual abuse

Warhol's talent and fame naturally attracted a large group of people: he had an entourage of artists, socialites, media and art-world folk, and general hangers-on around him, who all gathered at the Factory. Some of these people appeared in his films, and generally helped with his various projects. One of these was Valerie Solanas.

Born on 9 April 1936, Solanas grew up in Ventnor City, New Jersey. Her mother, Dorothy Bondo, eventually split up with her father, Louis Solanas, but before they did Valerie was the subject of constant sexual abuse by her father. When her parents divorced, Valerie found herself homeless, at the age of fifteen. Despite these difficulties, she managed to complete her high school studies, and then went on to gain a degree in psychology at Maryland University. In 1953, she had a son, David. During the 1960s, she led an unsettled life, becoming a prostitute and panhandler before arriving in Greenwich Village in 1966.

Solanas immediately gravitated towards the art scene in New York, and became a regular visitor to Warhol's Factory. The following year, she gave Warhol a play that she had written, entitled *Up Your Ass*, which drew on her experience as a prostitute. Some sources report that Warhol read the script but thought it was so pornographic he assumed that the police had set a trap for him – several of his films had been banned for obscenity. Whatever the truth, he did not give it back to Solanas, and when she enquired after it, making threatening phone calls, he admitted to her that he had lost it. When she asked for money in compensation, Warhol offered her a part in his film, *I, A Man* – unwisely, as it turned out.

'The SCUM Manifesto'

In the film, Solanas plays an aggressive prostitute who improvises a conversation with a client, expressing herself in a way that is at once surreal and full of obscenities. The same type of language is employed in her most famous work, *The SCUM Manifesto*. 'SCUM' is thought to stand for 'The Society for Cutting Up Men', though Solanas did not use these words in the book. However, the book was a violent diatribe against men, and women involved with men, that despite its sometimes nonsensical argument, found favour with the more extreme groups of feminists.

Warhol pronounced dead

Solanas was unable to find a publisher for the tract, and eventually published it herself. Meanwhile, she had become more and more infuriated by the fact that Warhol had turned down her play. On 3 June 1968, she walked in to Warhol's studio with a gun, and fired three bullets at him. One of the bullets went into Warhol's body, hitting vital organs, including his lungs. She then turned the gun on Mario Amaya, an art critic who was with Warhol at the time, and Fred Hughes, Warhol's manager. However, at this point her gun jammed, and she left the building. Warhol was rushed to hospital, where he was pronounced dead on arrival. However, he was alive, and miraculously, after several operations, he survived. For the rest of his life, his health was badly damaged, and he became reclusive as a result.

Solanas gave herself up, and was arrested and charged with attempted murder. From remarks that she made, it was clear that she was suffering from extreme feelings of resentment against Warhol, to the point of delusion, because he had rejected her work. She was brought to trial and convicted, receiving a three-year sentence only. Warhol himself refused to give evidence against her.

After her release in 1971, Solanas continued to be regarded by some feminists as a martyr for the women's movement. However, it soon became clear that Solanas was nothing of the kind; in an interview, she denied that *The SCUM Manifesto* was ever meant to be taken seriously. Her behaviour also became more and more deranged. She continued to harass Warhol until she was arrested once more. By this time, it was evident that Solanas was deeply mentally disturbed. The feminists lost interest in her, and she began her itinerant life once more, as a prostitute and panhandler, often spending time in mental hospitals.

Andy Warhol eventually died in 1987, aged fifty-eight, having undergone routine surgery for his gallbladder. Warhol had a phobia about doctors and hospitals, and for this reason had kept putting off treatment for his recurring gall-bladder problems.

He left a huge estate worth over $20 million which took nine days for Sotheby's to auction. The following year, Valerie Solanas died, aged fifty-two, of emphysema and pneumonia, in a San Francisco welfare hotel.

ADOLF HITLER

Adolf Hitler has gone down in history as one of the most evil rulers of the twentieth century, if not of human history. His rule of terror in Germany, in which millions of Jews and others were gassed to death in a programme of mass genocide, was so well organized, brutal and violent, that few had the courage to make a public stand against what was going on. Not surprisingly, there were many secret plots to murder him, especially towards the end of the Second World War, when it had become clear that the Third Reich was in a state of imminent collapse. However, there were only two major attempts on his life, neither of which succeeded.

Beer cellar blast

The first of these took place on 8 November 1939. This was the occasion of Hitler's annual speech to mark the Munich putsch of 1923, in which he had tried to seize power from the Weimar government led by Freidrich Ebert, and establish a National Socialist regime in its place. Hitler's rebellion was crushed, and he was sentenced to a jail term, but his sympathizers made sure that he was soon released. From that point on, he began his meteoric rise to power, supported by nationalists who felt that Ebert and his government had allowed Germany to become impoverished by agreeing to huge reparation payments after the First World War.

The putsch had started in a Munich beer cellar, and once Hitler became the leader of the nation, he returned there every year to mark its anniversary. In 1939, he returned to the beer cellar as usual, but this time the Führer's speech was a short one, and afterwards he left quickly, rather than staying to chat sociably to his friends in the party as he normally did. His haste on this occasion saved his life: twelve minutes after he and his entourage left, a bomb exploded behind the stage. It had been hidden in a pillar there, and within seconds, the whole room was blown to smithereens. Seven Nazi party members were killed in the explosion, and sixty-three people were wounded.

Torture, drugs and hypnosis

When news of the attempt reached Hitler, he became convinced that the person behind the plot was Neville Chamberlain, the British prime minister, who, he claimed, had instructed the British secret service to plant the bomb. Few, even of his most loyal supporters, believed this to be the case. Some cynical observers suspected the Nazi party itself, citing the example of the Reichstag fire. (In that episode, a fire had been started in the parliament building on 27 February 1933, and in the resulting chaos, Hitler and Goering had taken the opportunity to suspend many civil rights in Germany, blaming the communists for starting the fire. The event had marked an important moment in history for the Nazis, allowing them to gain political control in the country.) In the same way, some now believed that the failed assassination attempt was a ploy to gain sympathy for Hitler and the Nazi party, and that it had been master-minded by Hitler's henchmen, in particular

1939: Hitler visits the scene of the Munich bomb. He kept alleged bomber Johann Elser under continuous interrogation for years

Heinrich Himmler and Reinhard Heydrich.

The head of the SS foreign intelligence service, Walter Schellenberg, investigated the scene of the crime at the beer cellar and finally pronounced it to be a genuine assassination attempt. A man was arrested trying to flee across the Swiss border directly after the attack. He was a cabinet-maker named Johann Georg Elser, aged thirty-six. A Swabian (a member of a minority linguistic group in Germany), he admitted under questioning that he had set the bomb up, putting it into a pillar behind the stage, and fixing a complex timing device to it so that it would go off three days afterwards. At first, he claimed to have been working independently, but later he said that two other men had been involved in the plot, and had offered to help him escape; however, he swore that he did not know their names.

The Gestapo made every attempt to find out more, using their infamous combination of brutal torture methods, hypnosis and drugs, but Elser stuck to his story. Eventually, the SS officers who had interrogated him became convinced that he was telling the truth, and that he had acted out of genuine fanatical hatred for Hitler and his regime, rather than as a patsy for anyone else. Hitler, however, did not agree with his officers, and ordered Elser to be kept in a concentration camp throughout the war so that he could be continuously interrogated. Towards the end of the war, Elser was finally murdered by the Gestapo on 9 April 1945. His ignominious death was followed by that of his intended victim, Hitler, just a few weeks later.

Colonel Klaus von Stauffenberg (pictured) and other high-ranking officers plotted to kill Hitler in July 1944

The White Rose group: five students and a professor who were executed for producing leaflets which opposed the Nazis

The wolf lair

By 1944, it had become clear that Germany had failed to win the war and that the days of the Third Reich were numbered. Many of Hitler's former supporters now wanted him out of the way, so that once the war was over, the Germans could negotiate with the Allies on favourable terms, thus avoiding the complete collapse of German power in Europe for the foreseeable future. Accordingly, Hitler now became the subject of many attempts on his life: there were bombs placed on his plane, which failed to detonate; a bomb was hidden in his briefcase, but Hitler did not take it to the scheduled meeting; and three young men modelling Nazi uniforms hid bombs under their clothing, which would have blown them all up as well as the Führer, except that Hitler once again left early and the plan failed. In another instance, a bomb was placed at an art gallery where Hitler was scheduled to be making a visit, but once again, he left early and escaped death. By now, Hitler had taken to departing from his schedule almost every day, to avoid being the target of such attempts.

The next major attempt took place on 20 July 1944. It was organized by Lieutenant Colonel Klaus Schenk von Stauffenberg, the chief of staff to General Fromm, who was the head of the reserve army. Stauffenberg was known to be highly critical of Hitler. In private company, he often referred to the Führer as 'the buffoon', and had also been known to call him 'the enemy of mankind'. In so far as a Nazi officer could be termed liberal, Stauffenberg was a liberal, and managed to attract a number of officers around him who wanted to see a return to a more civilized Germany after the war.

Stauffenberg had access to Hitler's private headquarters, but never managed to plant or detonate a bomb there. Eventually, he decided to assassinate the Führer at his 'wolf lair', a wooden hut at Rastenburg, East Prussia, where he held secret meetings. On 20 July 1944, Stauffenburg attended a meeting there, with a bomb and a detonator in his briefcase. He put the briefcase under a table where Hitler was poring over a map with his staff, and then excused himself by saying he had to make a telephone call.

Stauffenberg hurried away, and as he did so, a huge explosion rang out. Convinced that Hitler had gone up in the blast, Stauffenberg jubilantly made his telephone call, telling colleagues in Berlin that the assassination had been successful. He even lied that he had seen Hitler's dead body, but many of the Nazis were cautious about the news – wisely, as it turned out.

Meat hooks and piano wire

In reality, Hitler had miraculously survived. What had happened was that one of the officers, while they were studying the map, had moved the briefcase out of the way, putting it at the back of a large oak table. The bomb went off, but it killed four men who were standing next to it. Several more were badly injured, but Hitler himself was hardly hurt at all. He suffered only from shock, some small burns and a blast to his eardrums. Once again, he had somehow managed to escape death.

When the news that Hitler was alive reached Berlin, Stauffenberg's colleagues breathed a sigh of relief that they had not acted immediately. Stauffenberg's boss, General Fromm, rounded up the conspirators and court-marshalled them, sentencing them to death. Many of the men involved in the plot were high-ranking officers, such as Ludwig Beck, the former chief of the general staff, so they were given a choice: they could either be executed or they could voluntarily commit suicide. Beck chose to end his life himself. Stauffenberg, however, was given no such choice. He was sentenced to be executed, along with several other conspirators. In true Nazi style, they were simply led outside, lined up against a wall, and shot by a firing squad.

Hitler's retribution was characteristically harsh, to the point of insanity. Thousands were suspected of being involved in the assassination plot, and none were given any right to defend themselves. Two thousand death sentences were apparently signed. As an example to others, Hitler ordered eight of the conspirators to be hanged 'like cattle'. They were herded into a prison cell and strung up with piano wire on meathooks screwed into the ceiling. In some cases, the men were naked. Hitler ordered a film to be taken of the event, which he later watched gleefully with his colleague Joseph Goebbels, who was said to have covered his eyes in horror as the images were projected before him.

In further retribution, Field Marshal Erwin Rommel, who had been to some extent involved in the plot, was ordered to take poison or face a public trial. He chose the former. General Fromm was also executed, for having behaved in a cowardly way during the attempt. Fromm had actually ordered some of the conspirators to be executed at the time, but this was not enough to save him.

Yet despite Hitler's vicious reaction to the assassination attempt, he knew that his own days were numbered. On 30 April 1945, as the Allies marched on Berlin, he himself was forced to admit defeat and commit suicide. It was the ultimate admission of failure.

MARGARET THATCHER

Margaret Thatcher was not only the first woman to be prime minister of Britain, she also held the post for longer than any other politician in British history. A towering figure in British postwar politics, the Iron Lady, as she was called by the Soviet press, had no shortage of fans or critics, but both camps would agree that she was one of the most determined leaders the country had ever known. She crushed the power of Britain's trade unions; took Britain into the Falklands War; raised taxes during a recession; and followed a policy of 'Ulsterisation' in Northern Ireland that elevated the role of the Ulster Defence Regiment and the Royal Ulster Constabulary in combating republican terrorism. Her right-wing approach to political issues made her extremely unpopular in some quarters, and she often sought protection from Britain's Special Branch and its corps of elite soldiers, the SAS (whom she referred to as 'my boys'). Thatcher went on to win every general election she ran in, and for many years it seemed that her regime would continue indefinitely. However, history was to prove that her autocratic, no-nonsense style of leadership had its weak points, and she eventually lost the support of her own party, and had to leave office as a result of their vote of no confidence.

Bomb blast

In 1984, the Conservatives met for their annual party conference in Brighton. The senior membership stayed in their usual spot: the Grand Hotel, one of Brighton's largest and most elegant hotels, overlooking the beach. The conference had already been running for some days when, at precisely 2.54am on the morning of 12 October, a large bomb went off. It was the day before Thatcher's fifty-ninth birthday.

Responding to the emergency signal received at the local fire station, firemen thought initially that a drunk had set the fire alarm off, as had often happened in the past. However, when they reached the hotel, they saw that a large section of the building's grand Victorian façade had been ripped off. There was also thick dust hanging like fog all around the seafront. As the conference was being covered extensively by the media, cameras arrived in time to see the survivors stumbling out from the wreckage, including the seemingly indestructible Iron Lady, who

Margaret Thatcher gets a standing ovation after her closing speech at the Conservative conference in defiance of the IRA

emerged blinking into the light. It appeared that she had been saved by her legendary habit of working through the night on her papers. When she appeared, she calmly bid the emergency workers, 'Good morning', and added, 'Thank you for coming.'

Apparently able to function on four hours sleep a night, at the time of the explosion Thatcher was working on her conference speech for the following morning, and so had left her room to consult with a colleague. On subsequent investigation, the explosion was found to have torn her bedroom to shreds.

The Provos

The Provisional Irish Republican Army were the chief suspects for the crime, and it came as no suprise when they released their statement later that day. Although the attack had been unsuccessful, it had come perilously close to its aim. The IRA's statement contained a chilling warning (now often paraphrased by the Bush administration when describing al-Qaeda): 'Today we were unlucky, but remember we only have to be lucky once. You have to be lucky always.'

Even though the IRA had missed their target, there were scores of other victims. Five people lost their lives in the blast, and thirty-four were hospitalized. The dead included Muriel Maclean, Roberta Wakeham, Jeanne Shattock (all wives of Conservative politicians), regional chairman Eric Taylor and Sir Anthony Berry MP. Mary Tebbit, the wife of cabinet minister Norman Tebbit, was left permanently disabled. These deaths and injuries were later justified by the

IRA as because the victims were what they described as members of the 'oppressive Tory class'. No comment was made regarding the eight-storey hotel's numerous night staff.

Despite official advice to the contrary, Mrs Thatcher delivered her conference speech that morning on time and as planned. 'This government will not weaken, this nation will meet the challenge, democracy will prevail,' she said. If anything, the IRA's action had increased sympathy for the Tory cause, rather than destroy the party's confidence.

Bomb in the bathroom

Forensics soon revealed what sort of bomb had wrought the destruction: a substantial amount of Semtex had been attached to a long-delay fuse, primed and then secreted behind the bath panel in Room 629. This had taken place three weeks before the explosion. Once police identified the room the bomb was placed in, and the date that it was put there, they were able to track down a registration name from the hotel's records. Of course, the name the guest had registered under was a false one, but there was a fingerprint on the registration card. Undercover operatives suggested a top suspect: Patrick McGee, the IRA's Chief Explosives Officer. The fingerprint was matched against prints found in a room in the Rubens Hotel in London, where a terrorist had attempted a bombing similar to the Grand Hotel, although the explosives had been found and defused in time. Clearly there was a single figure who was at least partially responsible and he had a consistent *modus operandi*. When the Brighton print was matched to

McGee, from prints that had been taken for a teenage driving offence decades earlier, the police swooped.

The 34-year-old McGee was arrested in Glasgow, and was brought to trial and convicted. He was given eight life sentences in prison. His trial was the focus of a great deal of media attention: after all, he had, perhaps single-handedly, perpetrated the biggest IRA bombing ever seen on mainland Britain.

The Brighton bombing acted as a 'wake-up call'. After the prime minister had come so close to being assassinated, there would henceforth always be a 'ring of steel' around party conferences and a much tighter security operation.

Aftermath

In the winter of the following year, despite her earlier rhetoric, Margaret Thatcher signed the Anglo-Irish Agreement, which conceded, for the first time, that the Republic of Ireland, too, had its part to play in the future of Northern Ireland.

While in prison, McGee successfully followed an Open University course that saw him gain a BA, and then a PhD. He was freed along with other paramilitary prisoners as part of the Good Friday Agreement in 1999, having served fourteen years, despite an appeal against his release by the Home Secretary Jack Straw.

After the passing of time, some of the victims of the bombing famously came to forgive their aggressor, even exchanging correspondence, and the daughter of murdered MP Sir Anthony Berry met him on a number of occasions, although it was

far from a meeting of minds. Patrick McGee remains unrepentant about his actions, and caused some consternation among locals (particularly Brighton's Irish community) when he revisited Brighton in 2004. The same year, by a bizarre twist of fate, the police raided the home of Abu al-Hindi, suspected of being the UK's top al-Qaeda operative. It was found that he had been living in the same flat that McGee had rented during the Brighton bombing twenty years before.

Luckily Margaret Thatcher managed to escape one of the most daring assassination attempts ever made on a British prime minister. On the night of the blast, instead of being tucked up in her bed, where she almost certainly would have been instantly killed, she was working into the night in a different area of the hotel, and so survived. Sadly, however, many other guests at the conference died or were severely injured, and there were also victims among the many hotel staff.

Whatever the IRA's ultimate aim in perpetrating the crime – and their statements, over time, became increasingly obscure – they did not blow up the prime minister, or intimidate the Conservative Party. Instead, they managed to alienate the general public from their cause, and increase respect for Margaret Thatcher and her government. At the same time, the bombing may have played a part in emphasizing the need for the British government to begin to recognize the role of the Republic of Ireland, which they did shortly after the event took place – a change of policy that is still being shaped.

Interior of the Napoleon Suite bathroom at the Grand Hotel, Brighton. Margaret Thatcher had left her room only moments before

BIBLIOGRAPHY

J. Bowyer Bell, Irving Louis Horwowitz (Introduction), *Assassin: Theory and Practice of Political Violence*, Transaction, 2005.

Lavender Cassels, *The Archduke and the Assassin: Sarajevo, June 28th 1914*, Frederick Muller Ltd, 1884.

Lee Davis, *Assassination: Twenty Assassinations That Changed the World*, Tiger Books, 1993.

James DiEugenio, Lisa Pease (eds), *The Assassinations:* Probe Magazine on JFK, MLK, RFK, and Malcolm X, Feral House, 2002.

Fabian Escalante, *CIA Targets Fidel: The Secret Assassination Report*, Ocean Press, 1996.

James Fetzer, *Murder in Dealy Plaza: What We Know Now That We Didn't Know Then About the Murder of JFK*, Open Court Publishing, 2000.

Hans-Bernd Gisevius, *To the Bitter End: Insider's Account of the Plot to Kill Hitler 1933-44*, Da Capo Press, 1998.

Greg King, *The Murder of Rasputin: The Truth About Prince Felix Youssoupov and the Mad Monk Who Helped Bring Down the Romanovs*, Arrow, 1997.

Adam Nossiter, *Of Long Memory: Mississippi and the Murder of Medgar Evers*, Addison Wesley Longman, 1994.

Michael Parenti, *Assassination of Julius Caesar: A People's History of Ancient Rome*, The New Press, 2004.

Carl Sifakis, *Encyclopedia of Assassinations: A Compendium of Attempted and Successful Assassinations Throughout History*, Headline, 1993.

Edward Steers, *Blood on the Moon: The Assassination of Abraham Lincoln*, University Press of Kentucky, 2001.

Peri Yoram, *The Assassination of Yitzhak Rabin*, Stanford University Press, 2000.

Websites

HYPERLINK "http://www.crimelibrary.com" www.crimelibrary.com a wide range of articles on assassinations and other cold-blooded killings

HYPERLINK "http://www.presidentsusa.net/assassinations.html" www.presidentsusa.net/assassinations.html analysis of assassinations of US presidents

HYPERLINK "http://www.aarclibrary.com" www.aarclibrary.com information on political assassination

INDEX